VINTAGE INDUSTRIAL

VINTAGE INDUSTRIAL

Living with Machine Age Design

Misha de Potestad
Patrice Pascal

RIZZOLI
NEW YORK

New York · Paris · London · Milan

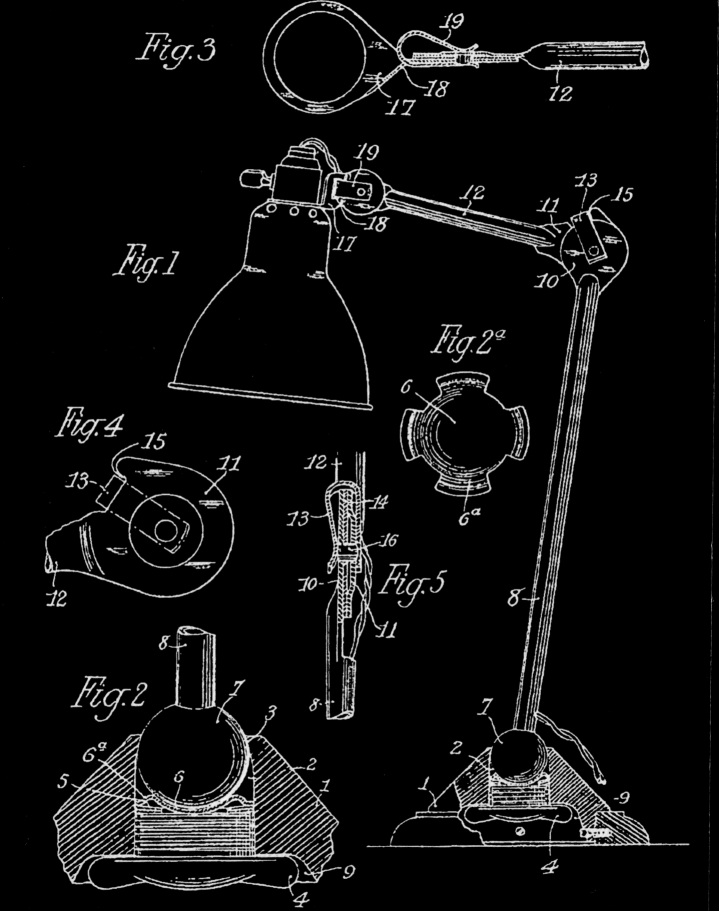

Fig. 3

Fig. 1

Fig. 2ᵃ

Fig. 4

Fig. 5

Fig. 2

PREFACE

The early twentieth century was a pivotal time in the history of furniture. The era's brilliant creations are indisputably the source of contemporary design, informing and inspiring today's designers, architects, and engineers.

A combination of unprecedented technological advances and creative spirit heralded the modernist movement in industrial equipment and furniture design. Industrial spaces, growing to house vast production facilities, needed fresh approaches to workplace organization. Innovators experimented with scientific and technical approaches to design, producing novel forms, systems, and devices to address the challenges of the rapidly increasing pace and volume of work in production sites—as well as the safety, efficiency, and comfort of the worker.

Engineers of this new, modern age may have taken their cues from the latest scientific studies, but they were viewed as artists—as Gustave Eiffel was with his controversial tower. Their art was expressed in designs that signaled the advent of an increasingly industrialized world; as machines began to dominate the aesthetic of an era of transformation, design became an integral part of this second Industrial Revolution.

Visitors to international expositions were awed by the magic of electricity that they discovered within lofty structures of iron and glass. Designers and engineers saw the potential of this new power source. Tasked to illuminate industrial and public buildings, they created dazzling innovations in the realm of lighting: ingenious configurations of prisms that intensified the light cast by lanterns in public spaces; adjustable lamps that could be installed, moved, and focused exactly where needed in workshops and studios; and even a medical lamp that has helped save lives by eliminating the shadows cast by a surgeon's hands.

Jobs in offices and factories multiplied and became more specialized. Designers addressed workplace safety and productivity by adapting furniture to all body types and work conditions. An adjustable chair that could pivot 360 degrees was designed for the convenience of typists. The cantilevered chair without rear legs was a turning point in the history of design, combining ergonomics and elegant simplicity, while mass-produced stackable chairs were economical to manufacture and freed up valuable space for productive use.

Factories, workshops, and offices all benefited from the expertise of engineers and their imaginative solutions. To accommodate an influx of documents and equipment, newly developed storage systems organized the work; tool closets and filing cabinets were soon within arms' reach. It became standard practice for equipment to be customized to accommodate the worker and facilitate the specific task to be performed; workplaces were now equipped with adjustable, folding, and stackable chairs, customized storage areas, and a variety of specially adapted lamps and tables. Frank Lloyd Wright effectively summed up the philosophy of the time: "Form and function should be one." Needless to say, this sentiment is a byword of contemporary design.

Early twentieth-century engineers and inventors merged artistic and scientific values. They inspired mechanization, new business specializations, and accelerated production methods to produce "intelligent" furniture with a rigorous economy of resources. These pieces derived their beauty from the balance and simplicity of their lines. Stripped of everything superfluous, meticulously designed to serve a specific function, they achieved an effortless beauty.

This furniture, both driven by practical requirements and mass produced, is a brilliant example of the significance and meaning of the word "design." As the philosopher Paul Souriau wrote in his book *La Beauté Rationnelle*, in 1904: "There can be no conflict between the beautiful and the useful. An object possesses beauty when its form manifests its function."

The precision of industrial furniture designed between 1900 and 1950 is documented in this book, which is not intended to be an exhaustive reference work, but to demonstrate the value of this legacy through photographic portraits taken in factories, workshops, warehouses, and homes. Acting as urban archeologists some antiquarians discovered these icons of a revolutionary period of innovation and now they are in the spotlight—freshly refurbished and as functional as ever. The wide variety and creativity of these products continue to provide a vast source of inspiration for contemporary designers.

MISHA DE POTESTAD

SEATING

MADE TO MEASURE

During the 1930s, designers were on a quest for improvements in workplace seating to promote higher-quality and speedier production.

Largely absent from factories and offices before industrialization, chairs soon became essential workplace furniture. Before the late nineteenth century, office work such as writing had been performed standing in front of a desk; there had been no chairs in workshops or around machines and drafting tables. The recent acceleration in the volume of work, and studies on posture and research into comfort, led to the creation of new seating. Initially, simple stools were introduced for artisans and the women working in textile mills and dressmaking shops. Still in rudimentary stages, these chairs nonetheless reflected the new impulse to fit the machine to the human worker; they were equipped with concave seats and backs, offered in a variety of heights, and sometimes came with rollers.

Machine tools that bent, stamped, and shaped metal accelerated the creation of innovative furniture that could be mass produced at minimal cost. Adherents to the modernist movement embraced this technology to improve on the work environment. The practical implications of their efforts are illustrated by the Bienaise—or "well-being"—folding chair that could be stacked for compact storage. In addition, in what could be considered the first example of modern production methods, engineer Joseph Mathieu used a stamping technique that allowed the mass production of a stacking chair from two rapidly assembled components.

Ergonomics—a scientific and systematic analysis of the human body in relationship to a designed environment—became a buzzword; designers and engineers dedicated themselves to studying the posture and movements of workers on the job. In keeping with the new century's ideals of public health and efficient productivity, machines were fitted to people's needs. Chairs could now be adapted to specific functions, being composed of discrete elements that would work in unison to function efficiently. Chairs were adjustable in height and could pivot 360 degrees on a central axis; springs brought flexibility to the user's every movement. This was the inspiration for Henri Liber, who used up-to-date scientific studies of posture to design the M42, arguably the first ergonomic office chair. When Mart Stam introduced his cantilevered design for a chair, seating made from tubular steel entered a golden age. These novel forms, which sprang from the innovative spirit of design pioneers, continue to inspire contemporary furniture. Their rational beauty corresponds exactly to the modernist philosophy.

Chairs stored in an antique dealer's restoration workshop await refurbishment and new homes. This impressive assortment includes some of the finest examples of industrial chairs: the Bienaise, Flambo, Multipl's, and Nicolle.

PAGE 9
The historic M42 chair designed in 1926 by Henri Liber for Flambo. The base is set on a central axis, and a spring gives flexibility to the back, whose height can be adjusted.

The pivoting Bienaise chair has an adjustable back and legs of tubular metal.

OPPOSITE
Minimalist and practical, the folding Bienaise chair, seen from various angles, is considered to be the first of its kind.

OVERLEAF
As contemporary seating in a converted workshop, Bienaise folding chairs fit naturally into daily life in this setting created by interior designers Michel Peraches and Eric Miele.

THE ELEGANT SIMPLICITY OF FOLDING CHAIRS

Bienaise, or "well-being," chairs made their first appearance in the early 1920s; their innovative design set the standard for simple, practical folding chairs.

The folding Bienaise chair is an icon of design. A simple and straightforward utilitarian object, fabricated from curved metal tubing and pasteboard, it was the perfect solution to the challenges of storage and mobility that arose with the implementation of twentieth-century, Machine Age concepts of workflow. The use of pasteboard to make the backs and seats may seem surprising, as the material evokes the ornamental objects of the Victorian era, but the material can be tough, resilient, and lightweight. The pasteboard was made by blending torn-up paper, glue, starch, and clay. The resulting paste was then molded and baked. Once varnished, objects made from it are impervious to wear and waterproof. The pasteboard backs and seats of chairs have withstood the stresses of hard use in factories and offices, the material's resultant rich patina now valued by collectors. The chair is a model of twentieth-century industrial furniture, and the Bienaise firm continued to design increasingly sophisticated chairs through the 1960s.

Sièges " BIENAISE ". Confort remarquable

Modèle pliant

Siège très solide et léger se pliant par un simple soulèvement de l'assise.

N° **187854.** — Modèle garni fibre. Prix : **85.** »

N° **187855.** — Le même, embouti, garniture simili-cuir havane, rouge ou vert.
Prix : **105.** »

Modèle tournant à dossier réglable

Siège idéal pour le bureau standard, dactylos, machines comptables, dossier et assise rembourrés feutre.

N° **187835.** — Modèle garni simili-cuir havane, rouge ou vert.
Prix : **225.** »

N° **187836.** — Le même, recouvert peluche grise.
Prix : **245.** »

N° **187837.** — Type fibre.
Prix : **175.** »

FROM TOP TO BOTTOM, LEFT TO RIGHT
*The support for a back made from pasteboard,
from the first generation of Bienaise chairs,
bears a riveted metal plaque.*

*Extract from a Mestre & Blatgé catalogue
of industrial equipment.*

*As the collection evolved, so, too, did the
materials and structure: flat and tubular iron;
seats and backs of wood, pasteboard, or fabric;
three or four legs, standard or extra height.*

Nº 926.150   Société dite :   Pl. unique

Établissements Biénaise, S.A.R.L.

Drawing included in the patent registered in Paris by Établissements Bienaise in 1946 describing a device that adjusted the height and depth of chair backs.

OPPOSITE
A newer version of the Bienaise chair in its original finish.

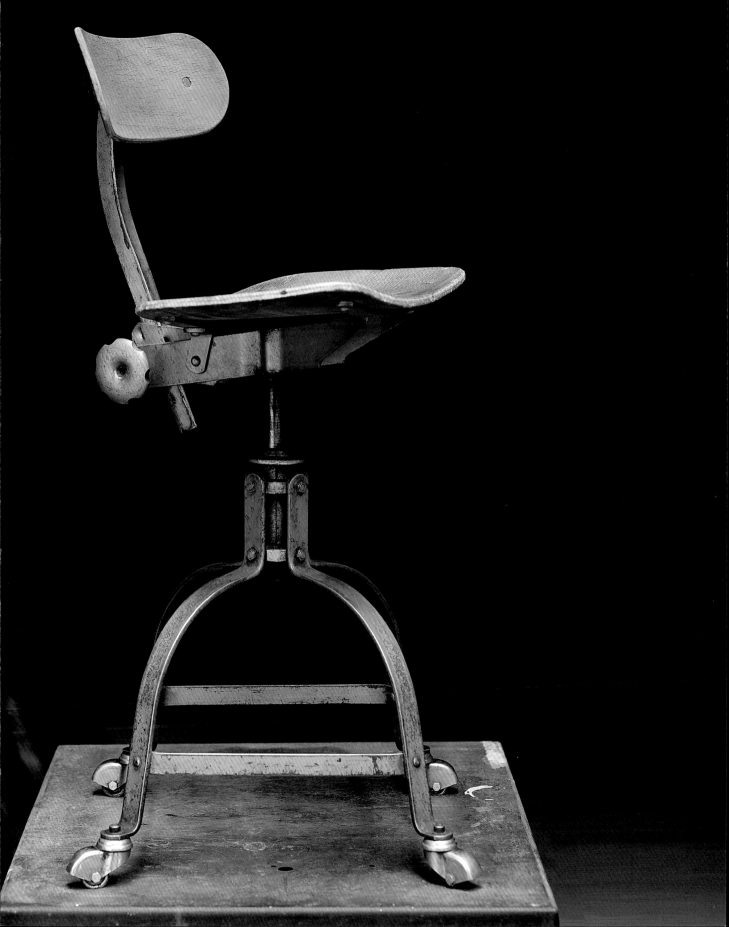

OPPOSITE
The 1950s Bienaise office chair stands out
in an architecture firm. The adjustable seat
and back are padded for greater comfort.

ABOVE
Quai aux Fleurs in Paris: Lined up in an agency's
office, Bienaise chairs are as practical as ever.
Here they hold pride of place and illustrate
the lasting appeal of the period's designs.

OVERLEAF
Designer Solenne de la Fouchardière and
the furniture and lighting firm Ochre have
turned a raw space in a former textile factory
in London into this bright loft. A concrete floor
unifies the wide-open area, and the imposing
kitchen unit, supported by a metal beam,
appears to float in midair. The Bienaise chairs
perfectly complement the scene, which retains
the spirit of the industrial building.

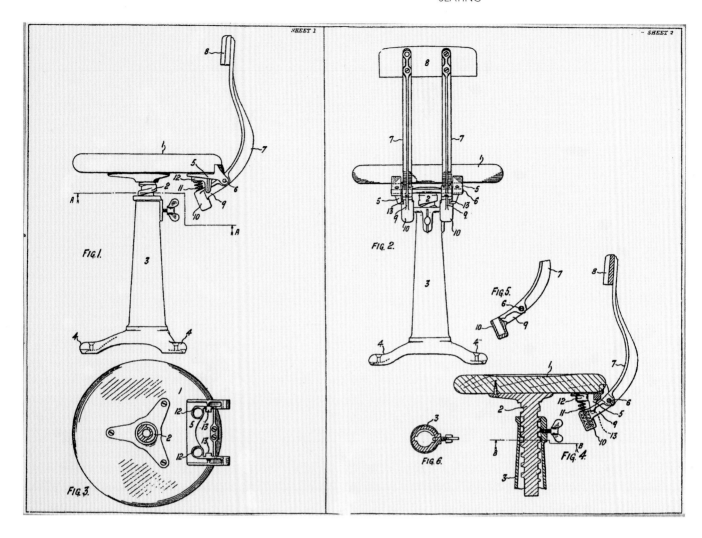

WOMEN AT WORK

The invention of the sewing machine revolutionized the entire textile industry, but the repetitive, fast-paced activity required changes in workers' seating.

In 1851, American mechanic Isaac Merrit Singer was already a veteran developer of inventions, including a machine for drilling rock, when he recognized that the sewing machines of his competitors would never be able to keep pace with the demands of the burgeoning textile industry. By replacing the clumsy rotary shuttle with a falling shuttle that stitched in a straight line, and incorporating a foot treadle rather than a hand-driven crank wheel, he created a robust machine that could handle the strenuous life of factory production. Dressmakers could now perform their work more rapidly and produce garments at lower cost. Women joined the industrial labor force in ever-increasing numbers, although there were concerns about the strenuousness of the long hours of repetitive work. In 1926, the Singer Manufacturing Company registered a patent for a chair intended for sewing workshops. Initially, the design was no more than a simple stool whose height could be adjusted; a back was subsequently added for lumbar support.

The plate of drawings above illustrates the patent registered by the Singer Manufacturing Company in 1926 in London.

The cast-metal column that serves as the
base for the Singer chair is hollow and can be
attached to the floor. A threaded screw controls
the height and is stabilized by a butterfly screw.
Springs provide resilience for back support.

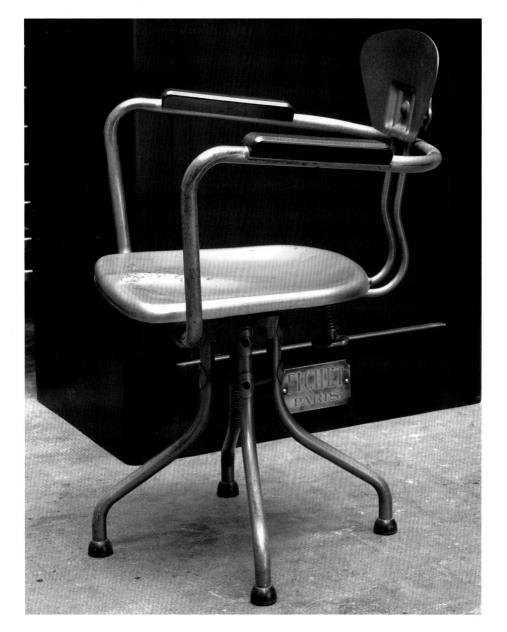

ERGONOMICS BECOMES A REALITY

Henri Liber's typist's chair is an influential predecessor of modern office seating.

In the 1920s and 1930s, Henri Liber registered numerous patents for office furnishings and supplies. He had invented a system for mounting shelving or drawers and sliding doors to close them, as well as exhibition easels, file cabinets on wheels, design instruments, and even a refinement of carbon paper. In 1926, he registered a patent for chairs that could be moved laterally, sliding on rails. When detached from its rail and standing independently, the M42 typist's chair combined all the functions necessary for facilitating secretarial work: its height could be adjusted, it could pivot 360 degrees, and a coil spring allowed the back to be tilted without its tipping over. In 1930, Henri Liber began to distribute his design under the Flambo name. The legendary M42 became an industry standard.

FROM LEFT TO RIGHT
Flambo armchair in its original gray-green color. A removable cushion was supplied for the seat and back.

Factory mark stamped on the back of the chair, above the adjustment mechanism.

The M42 ergonomic office chair designed in 1926 by Henri Liber for Flambo.

SALLES DE CONFERENCES

Installation complète de salles de cours, de conférences, avec bancs à pupitres.

Nous recommandons comme plus confortable l'installation avec fauteuils fixes indépendants, avec tablette pour écrire sur la droite du fauteuil.

200. D. Prix du fauteuil suivant détails de construction : **140** à **220** fr.

200 D

CUSTOM DESIGN

Studies on the well-being of workers became the basis for all industrial furniture design.

Conference rooms were furnished with chairs fitted out with desktops for taking notes during working sessions. In American industrial ironing plants, flexible chairs at each workstation were designed to improve women's posture. The seats of offices and workshops were equipped with a mechanism to readily adapt to different body types.

The Institut Alfred Fournier, a scientific foundation established in 1923, equipped its conference room with special chairs marketed through the catalogue of Établissements Jouan, specialists in medical equipment.

OPPOSITE
Made from oak and cast metal, this conference room chair could be attached to the floor, stand independently, or be part of a row. The small desktop made it easy for attendees to take notes.

LEFT AND OPPOSITE
Displayed here in the Galerie Duo in Paris, the Ironrite Health Chair in its original pale cream color. Its flexible structure responded to each movement and fostered correct posture in the worker.

ABOVE
Each chair is identified by a metal plaque on the rear of the back.

OVERLEAF
The ergonomic Health Chair, designed in 1938 to equip ironing factories in the United States, has over time been adopted for home use. In this apartment in Paris, the iconic chair accompanies a wooden cabinet with multiple drawers made for watchmaking workshops.

An American firm based in Detroit, the Sperlich and Uhlig Company, later the Ironrite Ironer Company, began to fabricate industrial ironing machines in 1918. The company then designed a chair to help women during their long hours working at these machines. The Ironrite Health Chair, developed by the firm in the late 1930s, reflected the newly popular scientific principles of ergonomics. The metal strips holding the lacquered plywood components allowed the chair to flex and spring, assisting the worker's every movement and reducing the physical exertion required to complete each task. This ergonomic chair was soon adopted for home use. It is now included in the Museum of Modern Art's permanent collection.

*Machinist's chair from Switzerland with
the K. Mischke, Sohn label.*

OPPOSITE
*Steel entrepreneurs and wholesalers based
in Stockholm, Anders Olson and John Odelberg
established a partnership to manufacture
this office chair. Produced by Knoll in 1947,
the T60U model is in Bordeaux lacquered steel
and birch laminate.*

OVERLEAF
*Adjustable and portable stools of unknown origin
provide seating throughout an artist's atelier.*

ECONOMIZING ON SPACE

The technique of stamping metal forms not only reduced production costs and increased output but it also encouraged the creation of innovative furniture.

Lyonnais engineer Joseph Mathieu invented a way to mass produce stackable chairs made from two pieces of stamped metal. To manufacture the forms, a piece of sheet metal was placed between a die, its two parts consisting of a mold and a relief punch. A powerful electric press forced the metal into shape by compressing it between the die. Mathieu's chair was fabricated through two separate operations, one for the legs and the other for the back. The two parts were then attached by rivets, with a seat made of wood or metal joining the legs and back together.

Between 1919 and 1922, Mathieu registered several patents for a system that allowed his chairs to stack easily and efficiently. A signature feature of his chair was its concave legs, which allowed chairs to stack closely together, valuable when space was limited. Distributed under the brand name Multipl's, these practical and sturdy chairs could be found in gardens and on café terraces.

Joseph Mathieu's 1920 design for the original stacking chair made from stamped metal. Multipl's were distinguished by the concave form of the legs, which tapered to a narrow point, allowing the chairs to be stacked easily and minimizing storage space when they were not in use.

OPPOSITE
Plate of drawings from Mathieu's patent registered in the United States in 1922.

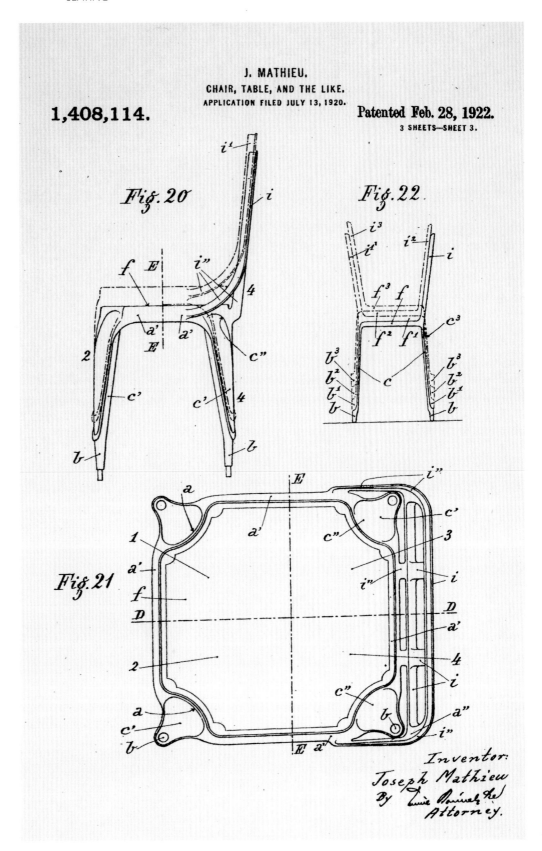

J. MATHIEU.
CHAIR, TABLE, AND THE LIKE.
APPLICATION FILED JULY 13, 1920.

1,408,114.

Patented Feb. 28, 1922.
3 SHEETS—SHEET 3.

Fig. 20

Fig. 22

Fig. 21

Inventor:
Joseph Mathieu
By
Attorney.

FROM LEFT TO RIGHT
Tolix stool after being stripped of its original paint.

The Tolix Chaise A, designed by Xavier Pauchard, featured convex legs to facilitate stacking and storage.

One of the first versions of Xavier Pauchard's chair design, dated around 1920. This model was not yet stackable.

The industrialist Xavier Pauchard recognized the possibilities of stamped sheet metal and, in 1934, he unveiled the Chaise A, also called the Model A, the quintessential bistro and brasserie chair. Produced in a factory in Autun, Burgundy, the chair was marketed under the brand name Tolix; unlike earlier stackable chairs, its legs were convex, making them even sturdier. Stackable and versatile, these chairs were as ubiquitous in French machine shops as public parks, and in 1935, they even sailed to America on the steamship *Normandie*.

Now in the collections of the Museum of Modern Art, the Centre Pompidou, and the Vitra Design Museum, the Tolix chair is still manufactured in the original factory in Burgundy.

First produced in a metal-stamping factory on the outskirts of Paris in 1933, the Nicolle chair was adaptable to all types of workstations, its distinctive form designed to meet the most up-to-date comfort and safety standards of the time. These stamped steel chairs were widely distributed to factories, workshops, and offices through industrial furniture catalogues that are themselves beautiful examples of the vintage industrial aesthetic. Discontinued in 1990, the Nicolle chair remained a cult favorite among collectors of vintage industrial furniture; it has since been reissued using the same manufacturing process and tooling as the original version. With its instantly recognizable "whale tail" back, the Nicolle, originally intended for industrial use, is now a stylish presence in domestic and urban spaces.

Original tools used since 1933 for stamping the very distinctive "whale tail" back. On the left, the relief punch; on the right, the hollow mold.

OPPOSITE
In an antique dealer's restoration workshop, a Nicolle chair and stool in front of a workbench, performing their original function.

In Paola Navone's Paris apartment, the very distinctive silhouette of Nicolle chairs, seemingly engaged in conversation.

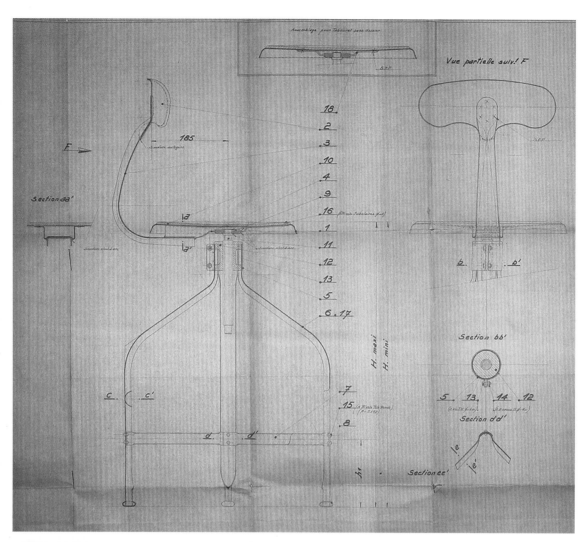

FROM TOP TO BOTTOM, LEFT TO RIGHT
*Blueprint of a pivoting version of the Nicolle chair
from the 1940s, showing the production details.*

*Raw steel chair backs lie in stacks before
being attached to bases in the manufacturing
plant in Paris.*

*In Jean-Marc Dimanche's contemporary house
in Paris, the repeating signature forms of Nicolle
chairs, reissued by the company MIJL, are a
graceful presence round a family dining table.*

Cantilever chair produced by Thonet in 1930. Based on a model made from plumbing pipes, this chair combines comfort and utility within its springy tubular-steel frame.

OPPOSITE
Evidence of Mart Stam's extensive research, this plate of drawings from the "Thonet Classic" catalogue is from the patent registered in Germany in 1929.

NOVEL FORMS

Tubular steel — a durable, flexible, lightweight material used in World War I airplanes — energized the evolution of the modernist style of furniture.

Inspired by the German Bauhaus, which preached an aesthetic of economy and functionality in the plastic arts, architect and furniture designer Mart Stam designed a radically new chair in 1926. Using gas pipes and ordinary plumbing connections, he created a spare, springy structure that utilized the principle of the cantilever to do away with two of the chair's legs. Soon this cantilever chair was fashioned from a material that epitomized the sleek, aerodynamic, modern look: tubular steel. Stam's audacious design inspired Marcel Breuer and Mies van der Rohe, who were also closely associated with the Bauhaus. Stam's simple, functional chair is still manufactured by Thonet.

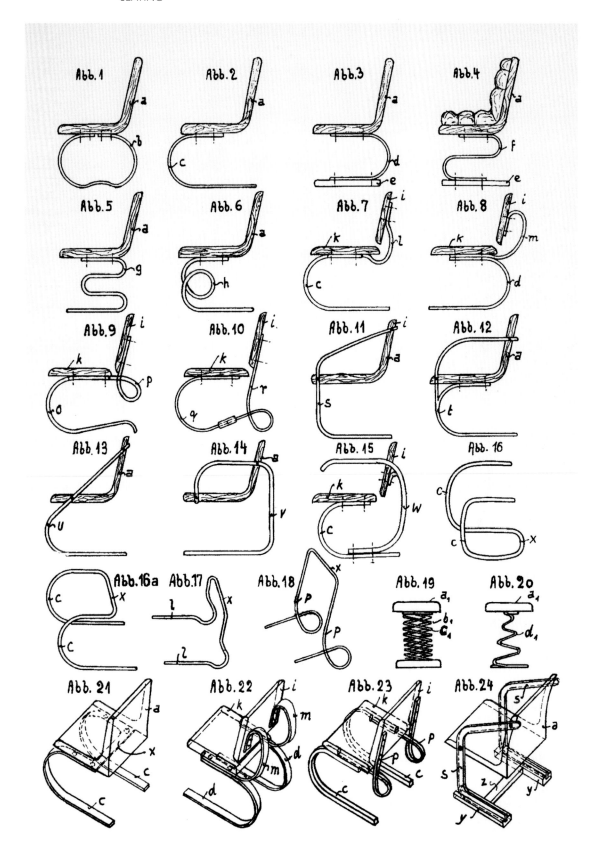

Mart Stam's design for the first cantilever chair called for a material that combined strength and flexibility: tubular steel. First utilized in World War I aircraft and automobiles, tubular steel caught the imagination of Stam, an architect with close ties to the German and Dutch modernist movements. Stam's chair was simple, functional, and lightweight, and users described the experience of sitting in it as like resting on air. His revolutionary chair reflected the Zeitgeist. Spare and streamlined, its silhouette fit perfectly with the architecture of the time. Designed to be mass produced, each chair was inexpensive to manufacture and affordable.

Thonet had established itself as a precursor of modern industrial design with its model No. 14 in the mid-nineteenth century. This bentwood chair consisted of a few standardized components that were delivered unassembled (the forerunner of today's kits). The method fostered its own revolution, quickly becoming accepted worldwide as a technique for efficient mass production. To this day, Thonet's catalogue features several versions of Mart Stam's cantilever design, along with chairs based on the same principle by Marcel Breuer and Mies van der Rohe. Tubular metal furniture is as popular now as it was when it was conceived, its machine-made, streamlined forms perfectly modeling the modernist aesthetic.

LEFT AND OPPOSITE
From every angle, the cantilever chair—displayed here in the Galerie Duo—has a silhouette that asserts both its utilitarian, industrial beginnings and its stylish aesthetic. Mart Stam's design in tubular steel, No. B263, was first produced by Thonet in 1932.

ABOVE
The manufacturer's discreet logo riveted to the chair's frame.

STACKED PRECISION

In the 1930s, a number of chair designs emphasized economy of space.

Surpil furniture first appeared in 1927 on the terraces of Parisian cafés and in the city's parks and gardens. Its designer, the industrialist and inventor Julien-Henri Porché, wanted to create the perfect stacking chair, one that could be stacked compactly and neatly, without ever needing to be forced together or apart. The chair's elegantly simple construction is worth admiring: two tubular metal pieces form a seat and a back, giving the chair both stability and lightness. But the Surpil chair's innovative design is most apparent when the chairs are stacked. Porché designed the angle and placement of the legs with such precision that, when stacked, an entire pile takes up no more floor space than a single chair. Functional, graceful, sturdy, and instantly recognizable, in 2012 the Surpil chair was reissued by the French company DCW, which also reissued the Gras lamp.

Surpil chairs by Julien-Henri Porché can be arranged in neat stacks to free up floor space.

OPPOSITE
The clean lines of Surpil chairs lend a refined yet casual look to a family living room.

Austere and elegant, the Tubor chair, attributed to Robert Mallet-Stevens, was distributed by the thousands at the Colonial Exhibition held in Paris in 1931. The industrialist Henri Hébrard established the Tubor brand and registered two patents in Paris in 1931. He claimed that this lightweight chair's leg configuration and the design of its back and seat would facilitate its fabrication and production as well as its storage. Hébrard even considered how to transport the chairs; patents describe a cart for safely moving the piled chairs.

The drawing accompanying the patent shows a chair with minimalist lines, which appealed to the architect and decorator Robert Mallet-Stevens. Mallet-Stevens's expertise in metal framing and enthusiasm for collaboration—he frequently worked with artists, musicians, designers, and filmmakers—meant he was a natural choice to develop the chair, and he was instrumental in refining its design and production. Mallet-Stevens went on to adapt the basic model created by Henri Hébrard for his own purposes. He included it in many of his decorative schemes for private spaces as well as for the exhibitions organized by the Union des Artistes Modernes, an association of architects and designers that he founded in 1929.

The lines of the stacking chairs above, designed by Robert Mallet-Stevens, echo the furniture produced by Tubor. They share simplified production methods and efficiently configured legs and seats that allow the chairs to be stored in a compact stack.

OPPOSITE
This tubular-frame chair was designed in 1950 by French interior architect and designer Jacques Hitier.

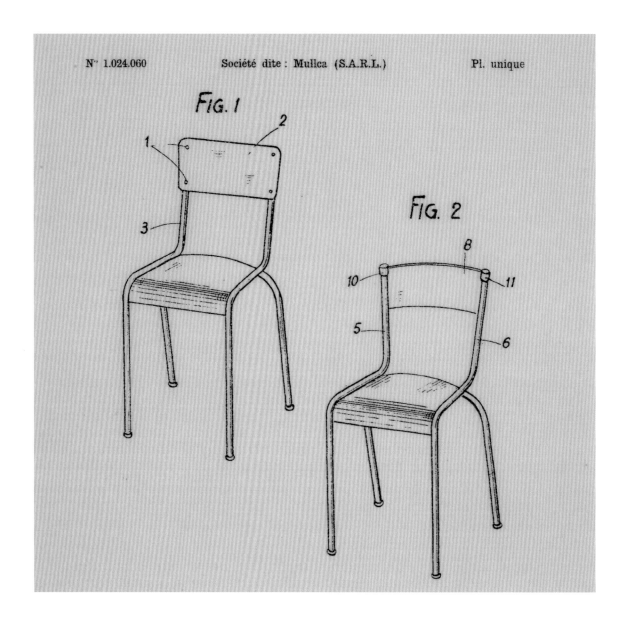

N° 1.024.060   Société dite : Mullca (S.A.R.L.)   Pl. unique

FIG. 1

FIG. 2

SPECIAL EDITIONS

The French Mullca school chair and the classic Emeco Navy chair, which has been a cornerstone of industrial design in the United States for 70 years.

The Mullca chair, created in the late 1940s, was a popular feature of classrooms in French schools. In the above illustration, figure 1 shows the patent for the original version of the chair designed by Gaston Cavaillon. Figure 2 illustrates the evolution of the seat and simplified method of assembly: the back includes grooves that slide in to make the chair.

In continuous production since 1944, the Navy Chair was designed for a life at sea. Produced by the company Emeco for destroyers and submarines of the U.S. Navy to be lightweight and corrosion-resistant, this now ubiquitous chair is made from a specially treated aluminum that is three times stronger than steel.

OPPOSITE
The cozy atmosphere of the eco-friendly store Merci, which occupies a former fabric factory located in the Marais district of Paris. Accompanying its spaces devoted to fashion and design, a café filled with second-hand books and furnished with industrial furniture and vintage Mullca school chairs welcomes visitors. A more sophisticated leather version of this chair is currently being produced by the company Ciguë.

Two examples of the III Navy Chair made
by Emeco in collaboration with Coca-Cola.
The III Navy Chair, so called because it consists
of III recycled plastic bottles, has exactly the
same measurements as the original aluminum
1006 Navy Chair designed in 1944. Still
manufactured in the United States in the same
factory, the aluminum seats were commissioned
by the government to supply American ships
and submarines with light furniture resistant
to water, salt and the harshness of life at sea.
The chairs are on display at Merci where
the furniture selection is a mix of vintage,
contemporary and reissued pieces. In front
of the industrial 1950s cabinets, steel Tolix
trestles and a fiber-reinforced concrete surface
make up the staff worktable.

TABLES

SCIENCE AND FUNCTIONALITY

The specialization of trades and the accelerated pace of production mandated changes in both office and factory furniture.

Using ergonomics, designers and engineers closely observed workers at their jobs, seeking to develop an optimal organization of space, machines, and workflow. Tables especially could be customized to adapt to the movements of the worker, notably to minimize repetitive movements and strain. Factors such as the position of the employee—does he or she sit or stand, for example—and the weight and volume of the materials used in the job were considered.

Tables made of cast iron or thick steel plates were set on casters or elevated with jacks to significantly reduce the physical effort of lifting and transporting even the heaviest of machines. The office also received an up-to-date modern makeover, often utilizing the smart, professional look of lacquered steel. Individual desks with ample storage space in drawers accommodated the growing volume of business and administrative correspondence, facilitating the work of the new professions of secretary and typist.

The engineers and designers who had introduced these cost- and space-saving features in workplaces utilized them in their own design studios. They invented systems that allowed them to control the angle and height of tabletops. Drawing apparatuses and parallel rulers were attached to the tables, sliding to follow any vertical or horizontal positioning of the surface.

These innovative tables, whether containing intricate mechanisms or heavy industrial-scale supports, are today rescued by visionary collectors to furnish architectural studios and office complexes.

A table that can be elevated with jacks to handle heavy loads.

PAGE 61
Detail of the mechanism for adjusting and securing the surface of Ferdinand Darnay's Classic drafting table.

UTILITARIAN FURNITURE

Equipment had to be mobile and durable to function in production spaces that operated on a vast scale.

Elevated tables mounted on rollers, lightweight portable tables, and massive cast-iron tables weighing several tons all contributed to the efficient progression of production materials from one machine to another, facilitating workflow and productivity.

A low table with a pivoting bottom portion for assembling mechanical parts.

OPPOSITE
Cast-metal drafting table intended for the machine industry has a rugged but beautiful presence in a spare space.

Athos cutting table for the textile industry. Ten feet (3 meters) long, it has mechanisms to control the surface angle and measure the fabric's length.

OPPOSITE
Industrial furnishings in a former atelier, now converted for residential use. A heavy wooden top supported by a cast-iron factory table base serves as a dining table. It is lit by Gras lamps and the Artichoke pendant lamp designed in 1958 by Danish architect Poul Henningsen for Louis Poulsen Lighting.

Aile d'Avion (Aircraft Wing) desk from 1940 in wood and folded sheet steel and a Standard chair in front of a soundproof partition made of folded sheet steel and perforated aluminum created for the refectory of the École Normale Supérieure de Cachan, a university in the suburbs of Paris.

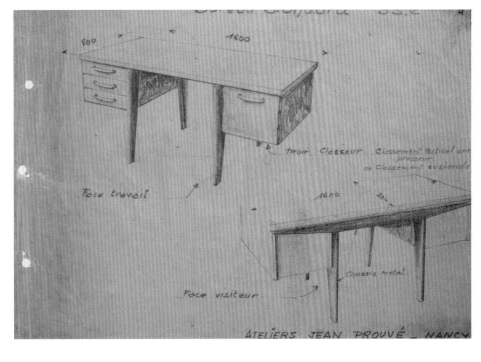

A page of a sketchbook from Ateliers Jean Prouvé in Nancy with an illustration of the Standard desk with drawers and cabinet.

JEAN PROUVÉ: MODERNITY AND HUMANISM

His creations in the field of furniture and architecture are exemplary and renowned worldwide.

Metalworker, blacksmith, engineer, self-taught architect, and designer, Jean Prouvé was a constant innovator. This modern man was also an entrepreneur. He founded his first workshop in 1923; architect Robert Mallet-Stevens was his first client and he later collaborated with Pierre Jeanneret, Charlotte Perriand, and Le Corbusier. In 1930, Prouvé helped establish the Union of Modern Artists and the following year he opened the Ateliers Jean Prouvé in Nancy. Inspired by the automotive and aerospace industries and harboring a keen interest in the public sector (Prouvé was elected mayor of Nancy in 1944), he designed furniture and building structures for schools, hospitals, and government departments in folded, stamped, and ribbed sheet metal. It was following these principles that Prouvé brought together the economy of means, strength, and capacity for mass production on which he based all his creations.

THE MODERN OFFICE

Modern office furniture was designed to showcase progress and efficiency.

Late nineteenth-century production facilities were woefully inadequate by today's standards. Space allocated to writing and record keeping was cluttered and unorganized; viewed as merely ancillary, offices were without basic comforts. However, a series of innovations at the beginning of the twentieth century transformed office work. Foremost among these was the Remington typewriter, first produced in 1873 in the United States and arriving in Europe at the turn of the century. This new writing device came on the scene at about the same time as carbon paper. Copies of documents multiplied, as did secretaries and office managers to file them. As administrative and marketing departments grew in importance, documents of all kinds—files, letters, invoices, receipts—proliferated. Soon even more employees were needed to manage all of the paperwork.

FROM LEFT TO RIGHT, TOP TO BOTTOM
A Roneo office desk fitted with a sliding tray for holding writing equipment with its original finish. A 360 lamp designed by René Herbst illuminates the desktop.

Extract from an advertisement for Artec, a specialist in office equipment, presenting a modern office installation that evokes order and competence. The typewriter and Flambo typist's chair occupy prominent locations.

Restored executive's desk in patinated steel.

PREVIOUS SPREAD
In the Jousse Entreprise gallery in Paris, a Pierre Jeanneret table is surrounded by Prouvé's Standard chairs designed in 1934 and made of folded sheet steel and molded plywood. The model shown here was released in the 1950s. The chair has since been reissued by Vitra. A Spider sconce by Serge Mouille illuminates the space, and a ceramic bowl by Kristin McKirdy sits on the table.

DESIGN STUDIOS

Intricate systems of counterweights and supports modernized traditional drafting tables.

Design studios, whether within companies or located on separate premises, brought engineers, technicians, and industrial designers together to develop and produce new products. These designers used drafting tables constructed to facilitate their work. Their surfaces could be adjusted with the help of counterweights, lifting pedals, handles, and fastening systems that provided stability. Attached to this support structure, a wooden drawing board was equipped with gliding parallel rulers that slid along a metal guide on either side of the table's top or drawing apparatus. The angle of the surface could be adjusted and customized for the designer's every position and requirement.

A page from the 1931 catalogue The Modern Design Studio, *edited by Ferdinand Darnay. He was the creator of the Classic drafting table, which is presented on the same page as the Unic table.*

OPPOSITE
Folding Unic drafting table designed by Lucien Sautereau in 1920.

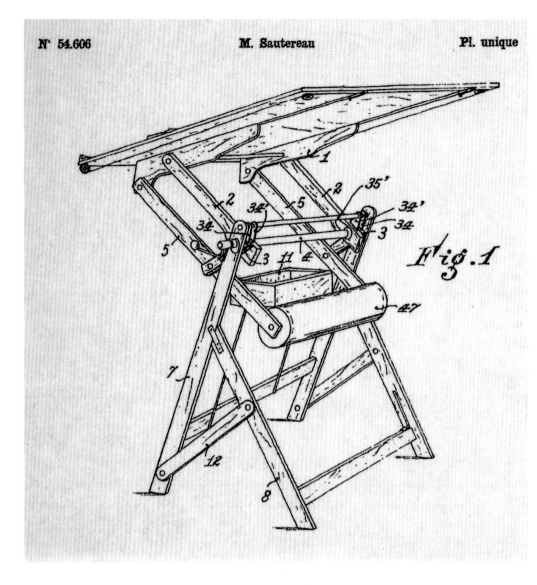

Fig. 1

Simple in appearance, with a distinctive "broken" silhouette, the Unic drafting table designed by Lucien Sautereau in 1920 is elegant in its conception. It features a wooden frame with two sets of folding arms that support the drawing board. Balanced by a counterweight and stabilized by a locking mechanism, the surface can be completely immobilized once its height and angle are properly adjusted. Folded, the table fits into a fraction of the space that the wide surface of the table's top usually requires and is easily transported. At the age of twenty, Lucien Sautereau designed and produced the first Unic in a workshop shed, achieving his goal of designing a simple table with "absolutely rational positioning." He continually made improvements to his invention and designed new tables under the Unic label.

FROM LEFT TO RIGHT
An extract from a patent registered by Lucien Sautereau in 1949.

From all angles, Sautereau's drafting table is an elegant solution to design studio challenges.

Logo riveted to the table.

An elegant yet playful composition of two
objects on a Swedish-designed table.

OPPOSITE
Cast-metal drafting table. The folding base
is integrated into the overall structure.

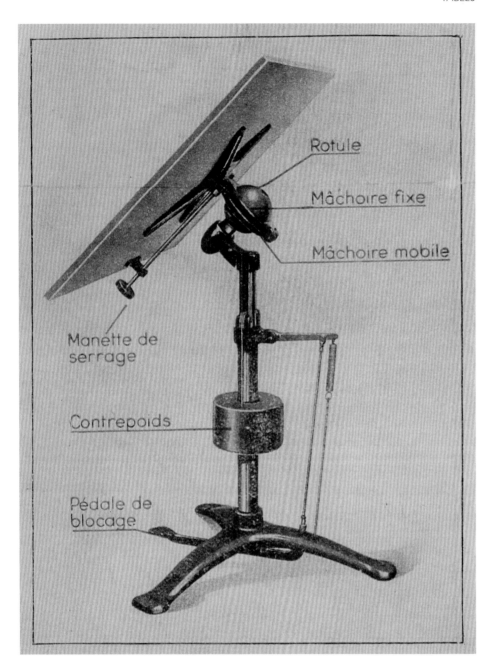

Rotule

Mâchoire fixe

Mâchoire mobile

Manette de serrage

Contrepoids

Pédale de blocage

INGENIOUS MECHANISMS

Refinements to drafting tables could look like works of art or be as simple as a redesign of a screw.

The Mappemonde drafting table won two awards at the 1932 exposition in Paris. The table stands on a telescoping central pedestal that allows it to be adjusted to any height desired. The drawing board can be turned and locked into the position required. The massive ball-and-socket joint, a block of cast metal in the form of a globe, is a distinctive feature and the signature of this remarkable table.

The Mappemonde, the only drawing board mounted on a ball joint, explained on this advertising piece from 1932.

OPPOSITE
A sculpture in its own right, the cast-iron globe and column form an elegant mechanism.

The Mappemonde drafting table in an artist's
studio. The clever configuration of steel parts
allows the user to easily adjust the angle
and height of the writing surface by turning
a handle. This intelligently designed table
is also a remarkable object of beauty.

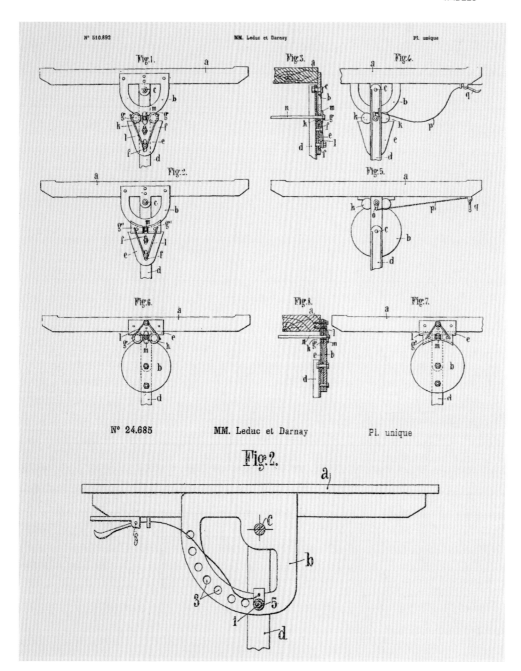

N° 510.892   MM. Leduc et Darnay   Pl. unique

N° 24.685   MM. Leduc et Darnay   Pl. unique

In 1920, the engineer Ferdinand Darnay and his partner, Maurice Leduc, registered a patent in the Industrial Arts category. Their invention consisted of a screw device that allowed the drawing board to be fixed in the desired position; its angle could be modified with a flexible cable and a hand control. In 1931, Ferdinand Darnay edited a catalogue in which he presented instruments and supplies for engineers and designers. His own designs were included, and there was a selection of special articles devoted to each maker. These catalogues read now like encyclopedias of design of the era.

Excerpts of several patent applications registered by designers Ferdinand Darnay and Maurice Leduc, describing the apparatus for adjusting the drawing board.

OPPOSITE
Ferdinand Darnay's Classic drafting table. The framework is made of cast steel, and the control apparatus is bronze. A counterweight and lifting bar facilitate adjustments.

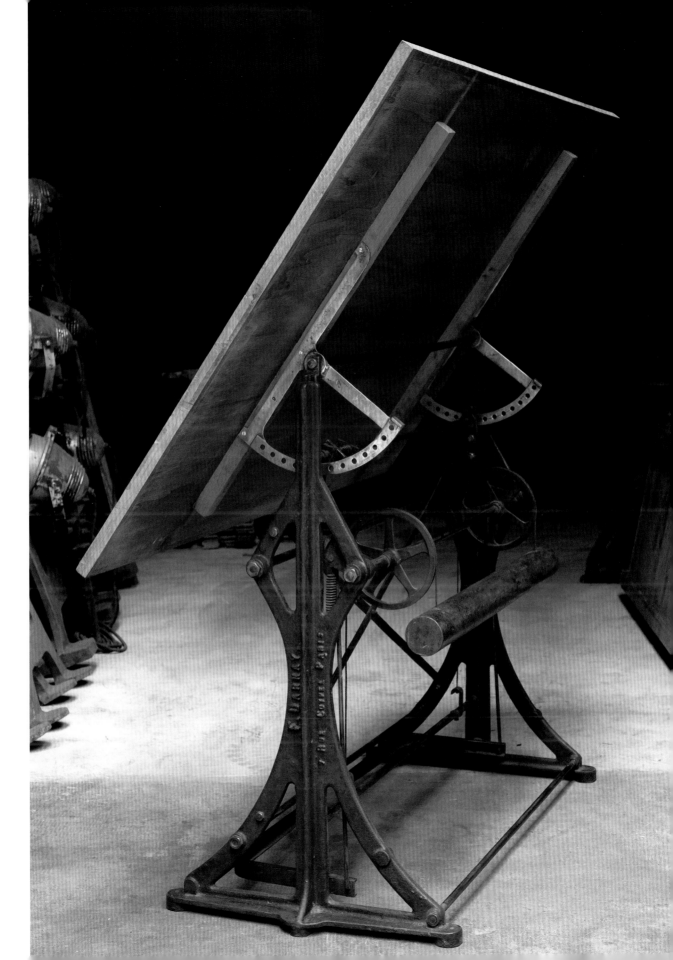

STORAGE

ORGANIZING THE WORKFLOW

As work and technologies became more systemized, they generated an unprecedented quantity of documents and records.

Filing, archiving, shelving—all of these activities became part of the workflow of mass production. The sheer volume of written materials in offices and administrative facilities alone required a standardization of materials and methods to organize and facilitate its handling—a challenge that designers met creatively and with scientific precision.

By the beginning of the twentieth century, the speed and efficiency of the Remington typewriter, produced by an American armaments manufacturer, eclipsed the use of pen and ink. Specialized schools offered training to the typist, which was a newly created office job. Even the paper sizes became standardized, the measurements changing to match the span of the typewriter's platen and the dimensions of file cabinets. Typewriters, equipped with carbon paper and onionskin, multiplied the number of copies of documents produced, which, in turn, compelled designers to develop even more space-saving, efficient storage.

Files for business records, as well as documents such as letters, invoices, order forms, and drawings, now needed their own furniture. Every workplace, from offices to factory floors, demanded filing drawers and cabinets, closets, and shelving.

Factories and workshops especially required major installations to facilitate the handling and shelving of materials and the warehousing of merchandise. Prefabricated assembly and standardized construction methods allowed these installations to be executed rapidly and cheaply. Metal furniture, sturdy enough to withstand rough handling, was tailored to use every available inch of space. Tool cabinets, storage racks, adjustable shelving systems, closets, drawers, and lockers became common features of workplaces.

Enterprising antique dealers have rediscovered this furniture in its original finish, sometimes covered in rust. Its beauty is revealed afresh after a sojourn in restoration workshops.

Stored in a restoration workshop, lockers, tool chests, and office file cabinets await the restorer's careful attention.

PAGE 87
Detail of a safe with a semicircular external bronze lock, the signature of Banque de France furnishings. Two managers were required, each with a key, to unlock the door.

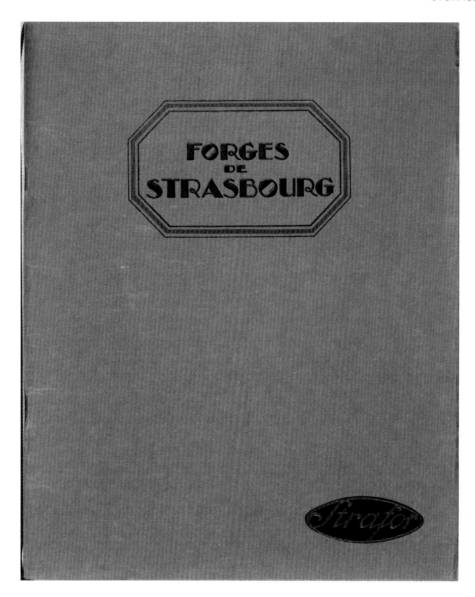

MODERNITY AND INNOVATION

*The modern approach to organizing offices, factories, and businesses emphasized flexibility
and accessibility, stimulating a wide array of innovations.*

Sturdy yet light metal shelves are now commonly found in workplaces, but in the early part
of the twentieth century, these shelves were an inventive solution to a surging demand
for updated factory and office furniture. Established in 1919, Forges de Strasbourg was
a pioneer in the fabrication of metal furniture. A leading producer of steel furniture in the
French market, Forges de Strasbourg first specialized in high-quality, lightweight sheet metal.
Then, in 1926, it established a furniture division, marketing its designs under the Strafor
brand, a contraction of the plant's full name. The firm's inventive use of steel expedited
fabrication of the metal shelves and provided flexible storage solutions at the lowest possible
cost. In 1974, Strafor merged with the American company Steelcase, which continues
to build on Strafor's longstanding expertise in the field of office installations.

*Cover of the 1926 Forges de Strasbourg
catalogue. Its Strafor brand would become
recognizable worldwide.*

OPPOSITE
*Mass-produced Strafor file cabinet with
drop-down doors, which could be used
as shelves for reviewing documents.*

FACULTÉ DE DROIT DE PARIS - INSTALLATION A 3 ÉTAGES

UN DES ÉTAGES AVEC PLANCHER A CLAIRES-VOIES

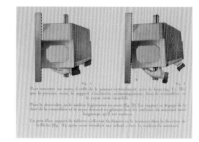

The Strafor system was a model of accommodation; its adjustable shelves were connected to racks that could be installed against a wall or in the middle of a work space, with two units placed back to back. Its standardized and detachable pieces readily adapted to a multitude of organizational needs and facilitated easy access to documents and inventories. Impeccably designed, the mass-produced Strafor shelf systems were made of steel sheets, kiln-glazed at a very high temperature. The components were delivered unassembled—the concept of a "kit" having already been introduced by Thonet in the middle of the nineteenth century. Strafor's cupboards and file cabinets, with drop-down doors or drawers, were also designed to be mass produced and assembled easily. The simple lines of this innovative furniture are complemented by bronze handles and label holders, the decorative signature of the Strafor brand.

FROM LEFT TO RIGHT
Example of a Strafor installation in a law school in Paris.

Two sketches of methods for installing and adjusting shelving from the 1926 Forges de Strasbourg catalogue. The spacing between the shelves could be adjusted in increments of ⅝ inch (1.5 centimeters) without removing the contents.

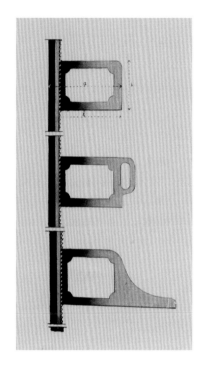

Strafor shelving racks, flawless in design, could adapt to a multitude of organizational needs.

OVERLEAF
Illustrations from the Forges de Strasbourg catalogue showing installations that have been carried out all over the world: the preliminary workshop preparation for a major structural installation (p. 94); an arrangement suitable for storage of archives at a site in Belgium (p. 95).

MONTAGE PRELIMINAIRE A L'ATELIER

SOCIÉTE DE TRANSPORTS ET D'ENTREPRISES INDUSTRIELLES A BRUXELLES

REFINEMENTS

Designers of storage furniture modernized drop-down doors and drawers with meticulous attention to detail.

Handles, label holders, and metal fittings were often the only items that could distinctively identify the products of each manufacturer. Distinguishing marks ranged from simple buttons to petal-shaped drawer pulls made of copper or steel. A narrow border of gold paint on the front of the piece could serve as a discreet, elegant signature. Designers modernized closing and locking mechanisms on office equipment. The rolltop desk, originally an eighteenth-century design, was completely reinterpreted. In the updated version, articulated steel rolled around an axis set into the upper part of the piece. This "curtain-style" roll-down closure system had originally been used for desks handcrafted from rare woods, but it was now featured in large production runs.

Notary's storage cabinet with a roll-down metal curtain.

OPPOSITE, FROM TOP TO BOTTOM
Metal chest of drawers directly inspired by traditional wooden furniture.

Detail of the drop-down door of a Strafor filing cabinet, with bronze ornamentation and a petal-shaped pull.

PREVIOUS SPREAD
In her Paris apartment, Paola Navone has incorporated a factory storage locker to store dishes and leftovers.

The polished brass lock and handle of the safe that used to be found in all of the branches of the Banque de France.

OPPOSITE
Between 1910 and 1930, the Banque de France used identical furniture, designed by the architect Alphonse Defrasse, in all of its branches. The pieces were installed as the central bank constructed its buildings across the country. This metal cabinet now on display at Quintessence in Paris was originally used to securely store worn-out banknotes that would be subsequently destroyed. The sliding doors are fitted with semicircular locks specially designed by the architect's team.

SECURITY MEASURES

Protecting valuables and documents became a job for heavy steel furniture with sophisticated mechanisms.

Armored cupboards, safes, and filing cabinets, equipped with locks and highly sophisticated systems of access codes, had become standard business equipment. Often resembling traditionally styled domestic furnishings, these office pieces were interpretations of cupboards, chests, and consoles but fabricated from heavy steel. They were massive objects, usually embellished with details like moldings and polished bronze pulls. This furniture was intended for banks, medical facilities, and important administrative offices.

FROM LEFT TO RIGHT
*An austere-looking safe dating from about
1900, fabricated by P. Haffner & Cie
in Sarreguemines, in northeastern France.*

*Safe manufactured by Klinger with a protective
casing of heavy steel, accessed only by a code.*

Notary's cabinet secured with a cylindrical metal roll-down curtain, showing the stacked rows of drawers.

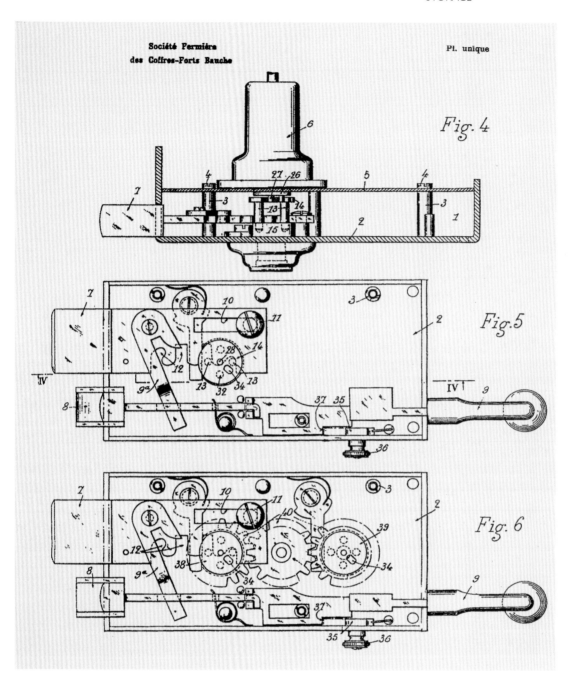

Société Fermière
des Coffres-Forts Bauche

Pl. unique

Fig. 4

Fig. 5

Fig: 6

*Sheet of drawings illustrating the patent filed
in 1928 by the Société Fermière des Coffres-
Forts Bauche for an advanced lock mechanism.
The company Fichet-Bauche has been a leader
in secure storage since 1825.*

OPPOSITE
*A barge moored on the banks of the Seine,
in the heart of Paris, renovated with doors
from a factory boiler room.*

INDIVIDUAL SPACE

Rapid growth in industry triggered an influx of factory, workshop, and office staff — all of whom needed space to store their belongings.

Business owners began to provide individual lockers for employees, so that laborers could store their personal effects and change their clothing at the beginning and end of their shifts. With its collection of seven types of metal lockers, Strafor had storage possibilities for every type of business. Durability was of paramount importance. Strafor lockers were made of the sturdiest, smoothest metal plate, a material its catalogue proclaimed to be cleaner and more hygienic than wood. They could easily be wiped clean, and had space to hang garments so that they did not require folding. Each locker was fastened with a padlock. There was even a model especially made for women; it had enough space for fashionable ladies to store large-brimmed hats. Steel was now the consummate modern material for furniture.

Fluted steel plate Strafor locker from ca. 1930 with anonymous factory stools.

OPPOSITE
With its handsome gunmetal-gray finish, this restored locker is ready for a new life.

FROM LEFT TO RIGHT
A Belgian locker with a distinctive label holder, padlock closure, and upper and lower openings for ventilation. A collection of anti-explosion lamps with metal guards is placed on top of the locker.

The chic Chinese-red lacquered interior of a locker following its restoration.

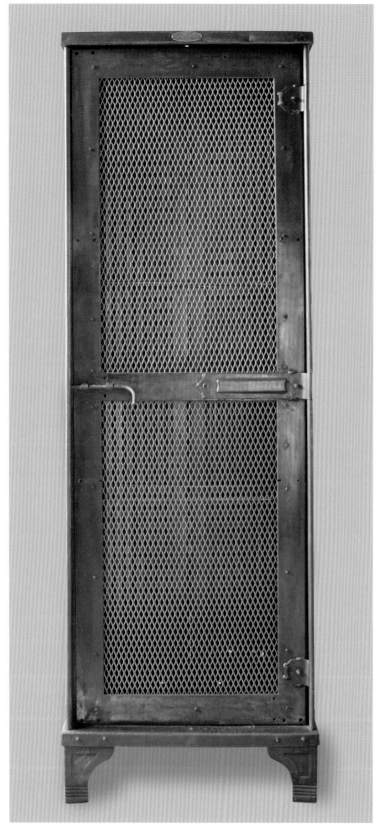

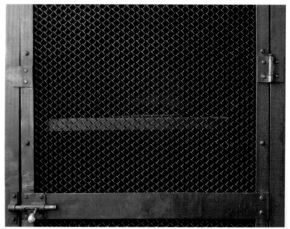

*Tool cabinet and details of the metal mesh used
for its door. Originally a pragmatic response
to the need for ventilation, the mesh and its
intricate interweaving strands lend a clean,
machine-made aesthetic to modern spaces.*

STRETCHING STEEL

The quantity of tools grew exponentially in this newly industrialized world; customized metal furnishings stored prized equipment and essential supplies in a safe and secure location.

Metal locker doors and tool cabinets were secure and sturdy, but workers needed to be able to see where their supplies were kept. Introduced in 1902, a technique of cutting and stretching a piece of sheet metal created wire mesh. This mesh permitted light and air into what would otherwise be a dark and stifling space—also important for the storage of food for meals. A simple metal grill could also serve this function, with a latch or padlock for closure. Whether as a single unit or stacked in multiples, these containers allowed each worker to safeguard his personal collection of tools, familiar to his hands and responsive to their skilled touch. These units were located in the middle of workshops, as well as in lunchrooms to hold the food brought by each worker for lunch breaks.

A cabinet with drawers and wire-mesh doors in a contemporary Parisian restaurant.

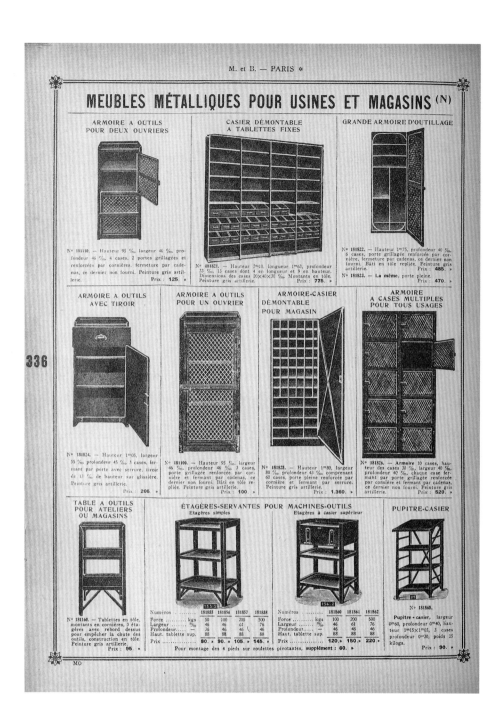

A page from the catalogue of Mestre & Blatgé, specialists in industrial equipment, showing a range of openwork cabinets and shelving units for tools.

OPPOSITE
A unit of stacked, numbered wire-mesh cabinets, designed to be sealed with padlocks.

Photographed in their original finish, sheet-metal transport cases used to store metal pieces for manufacturing.

A bin made of pasteboard on rollers, utilized to transport Suroy brand textiles in the factories of northern France.

TAILOR-MADE STORAGE

Containers, bins, and racks transferred materials and merchandise at high volume within warehouses and factories.

Steel bins and racks fitted with handles, labels, and rollers were robust enough to stand up to the hardest wear. Some were perforated for soaking in the special chemical baths required for treating metal components. The textile industry used pasteboard bins that could safely hold delicate fabrics. While waiting to be delivered or used within a company, tools and merchandise were stored on the shelves that lined the walls of production sites.

FROM LEFT TO RIGHT
A loft's need for storage remedied by burnished steel crates used to transport food in airplanes. The panel in pressed metal is a trompe l'oeil element that mimics the stucco ceilings.

Perforated steel bins used to transport and soak metal pieces that were treated in successive chemical baths.

UNLIMITED LIFESPAN

Metal industrial furniture was designed to withstand hard wear over extended periods of time.

Metal cabinets and chests—the bigger the better—were essential furniture in workshops. The broad assortment of tools required for working in wood or metal each found a place in the numerous drawers of well-designed cabinets; even their tops could serve as work surfaces. Storage cabinets, reinforced at edges, corners, and hinges, could be further secured with heavy padlocks. Practical and built to last, these massive pieces had to protect their contents when transported from one work site to another.

Stored in an antique dealer's atelier and bearing unmistakable traces of their former life, these work chests were used by the French army in its military workshops.

OPPOSITE
Now restored, this piece of furniture with military origins is now ready for use in civilian life.

Large reinforced cabinet with locks for the storage of merchandise, displayed at the Saint-Ouen flea market in Paris.

A massive storage cabinet made of steel sheet metal with multiple drawers to organize documents, tools, and replacement parts in workshops and offices.

Storage cubbies from a metal fabrication factory
are a perfect fit for a contemporary kitchen.

OPPOSITE
Salvaged by an events coordinator, a wall of
containers for storing and organizing light bulbs
used in party decorations.

LIGHTING

PROGRESS AND DESIGN

The entrepreneurial spirit of the period's engineers and inventors produced major advances in lighting.

Paris emerged from the shadows when gas lamps were installed in 1840 on the place Vendôme and the rue de la Paix. By the end of the century, thousands of gas street lamps illuminated the capital's streets—the origin of Paris as the mythical "City of Lights."

Then a new energy source, electricity sparked the conversion of the gas-powered cast-iron lanterns that lined urban streets in major cities. The opening of the 1900 Universal Exposition and the Parisian Métro system, constructed to alleviate traffic congestion, were perfect opportunities for showcasing this new technology. At the entrances of stations, rows of glowing Holophane lamps in porthole-esque fixtures lit the steps leading to the platforms. Manufactured from prismatic glass, then a new invention, these brilliantly lit globes illuminate the entrances of most Parisian Métro stations today.

In one of the first crossovers from industrial design to interior design, engineer Bernard-Albin Gras developed a line of innovative lamps that quickly gained a cult following, including a nod of approval from Le Corbusier, who exclusively used Gras lamps in his own offices. An ingenious task lamp was created in the United Kingdom under the brand name Anglepoise; it remains a coveted design. Lighting became mobile, adjustable, and adaptable—perfectly suited to the fast-paced modern era.

In the spirit of modernism, electricity, a source of efficient power and reliable light, was viewed as the key to the advancement of society. Raoul Dufy executed the largest painting of the twentieth century for Robert Mallet-Stevens's Palais de la Lumière, a structure built for the 1937 Universal Exposition in Paris. *La Fée Électricité* was a paean to progress. Dufy depicted all the scholars and scientists who figured in the history of electricity, life-size, on a canvas that measured 33 feet by 197 feet (10 by 60 meters). Coal had fueled the first Industrial Revolution, but electricity powered the second Industrial Revolution in the twentieth century.

Holophane lighting fixture for use in factories and public spaces made of painted sheet metal with a prismatic molded-glass diffuser.

PAGE 125
Jieldé fixture on the wall of a Parisian brasserie.

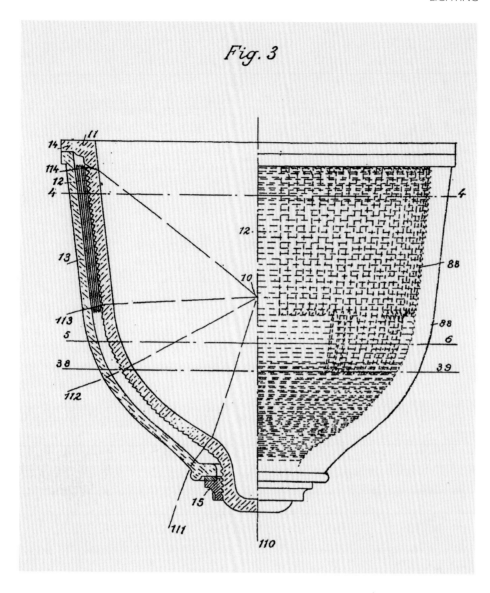

Fig. 3

Detail of a drawing for a patent registered in 1923 by the French company Holophane. A cross section of prismatic glass designed to intensify a source of light.

OPPOSITE
Porthole-shaped cast-aluminum Holophane fixture with a molded-glass globe. Designed in 1900 to light the entrance to Parisian Métro stations, these lamps are still used in Métro stations today.

OVERLEAF
Freed of their metal casings, molded-glass Holophane globes illuminate the dining room table in Paola Navone's Paris apartment.

THE SCIENCE OF PERFORMANCE

Mass-production methods demanded maximum performance from industrial lighting.

More efficient and adaptable lighting became a necessity in industrial work spaces and offices after the second Industrial Revolution. The widespread availability of electricity fostered inventive solutions that ranged from fixtures to globes. Early twentieth-century engineers applied their scientific training to developing lighting that played a decisive role in the fast-paced industrial expansion.

How to disperse light effectively was one challenge. As early as 1893, André Blondel, a French scientist, and Spiridion Psaroudaki, a Greek engineer, invented a light diffuser fashioned from molded glass, based on the principle of a Fresnel lens. Their glass globe, with its complex arrangement of prisms that scatter and intensify the source of light, is the basis of Holophane glassware. Its crisp, clean lines are the epitome of the early twentieth-century industrial aesthetic.

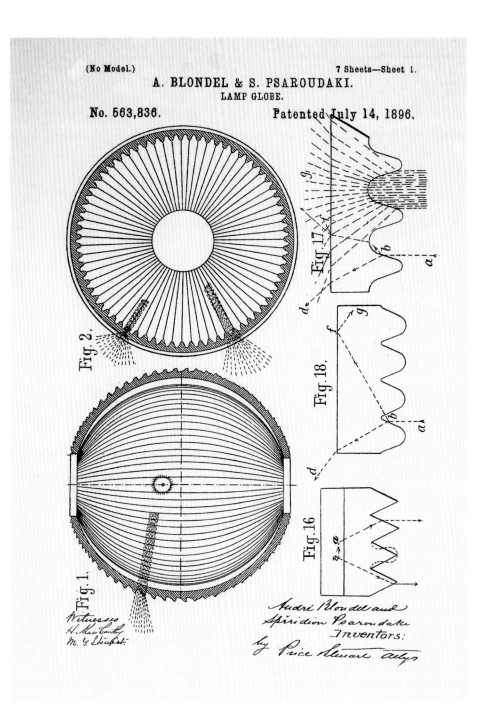

(No Model.)   7 Sheets—Sheet 1.

A. BLONDEL & S. PSAROUDAKI.
LAMP GLOBE.

No. 563,836.   Patented July 14, 1896.

A plate of drawings from a patent registered by the designers André Blondel and Spiridion Psaroudaki in the United States on July 14, 1896. Figure 1: Vertical section of a globe designed for an arc lamp; the exterior grooves reflect and refract light to all parts of the globe. Figure 2: Horizontal section showing the form of the interior grooves, and the distribution and refraction of light by the globe's internal prisms.

OPPOSITE
The company name, "Holophane France," stamped in relief on the rim of the globe, with the grooves of the glass shown in detail.

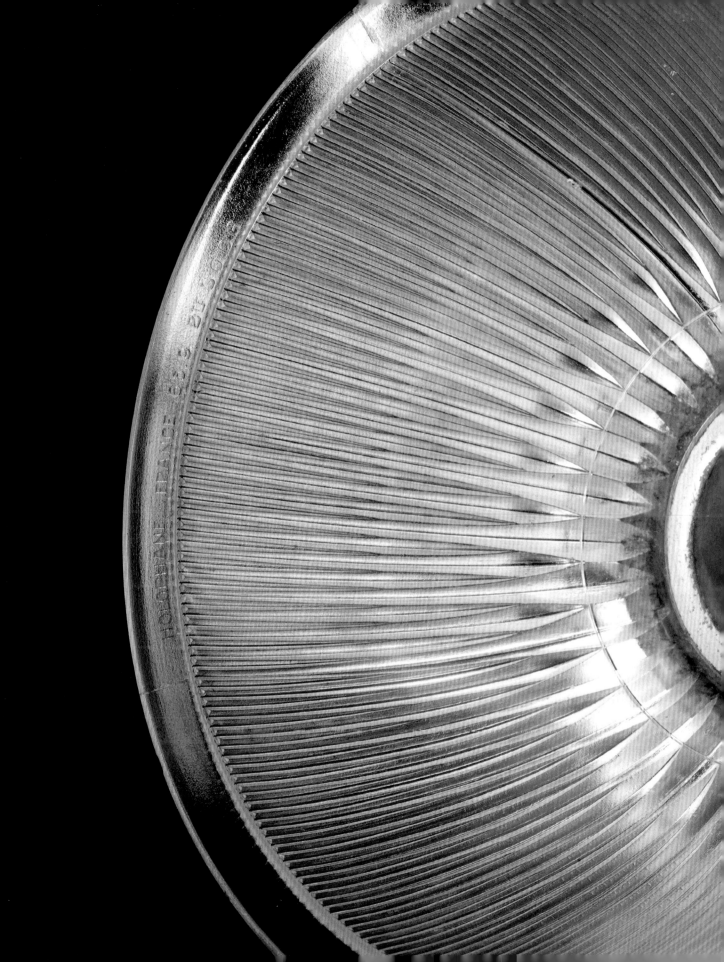

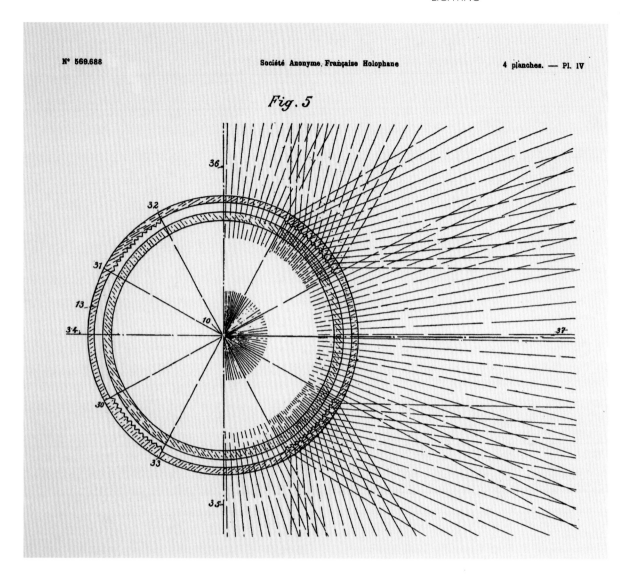

N° 569.688   Société Anonyme, Française Holophane   4 planches. — Pl. IV

Fig. 5

THE LUMINESCENT GLOBE

How to intensify a source of light is an age-old challenge; in 1893, combined luminosity and efficiency became a reality.

André Blondel and Spiridion Psaroudaki registered patents for their light diffuser all over the world. Patent No. 563.836, filed in the United States Patent Office in July 1896, included seven pages of complex calculations and drawings that illustrate how the globe's tiny prisms reflect and refract light rays. The globe's luminous effect, achieved with no loss of electrical efficiency, is attributable to its arrangement of prisms in the form of grooves and ribs on the interior and exterior of its thick glass. These striations direct the light without leaving any area in shadow. The name "Holophane" was an inspired choice; derived from the two Greek words *holos* and *phanein*, it translates as "that which appears to be wholly luminous." The two men never exploited their invention commercially and sold their intellectual property rights to American industrial companies.

Plate from a patent registered in Paris by the Société Anonyme Française Holophane illustrating the trajectory of a ray of light.

Cast aluminum and copper projector lamp labeled with the Holophane name.

In 1896, Otis Mygatt established the Holophane Company in London; by 1898 it had grown to become the Holophane Glass Company, with headquarters in New York City. Banks, grand hotels, and prestigious shops equipped their public spaces with Holophane lighting. The invention returned to its original home in 1921 with the establishment of the Société Anonyme Française Holophane, which specialized in the production of decorative glass, automobile headlights, and lamps for lighting public spaces. After more than a century of profitable operation, the Holophane companies continue to market state-of-the-art lighting and optical products.

URBAN SPACES: PUBLIC LIGHTING

Holophane globes were originally intended for street lamps of major cities.

These luminescent spheres, measuring either 18 or 24 inches (45 or 60 centimeters) in diameter, each perched on an iron pole, appeared in the 1940s. The street lamps went out of production in the 1970s but examples can still be found, some of them lighting elegant present-day apartments.

The brightness of the light is enhanced by prisms engraved both on the inside and outside of the globe creating a beautiful lighting effect.

OPPOSITE
Antique dealer Martine Valli placed these globes of light in a Parisian home to showcase a spectacular factory staircase and elements of a cast-iron nineteenth-century veranda.

ADJUSTABLE FOR ANY PURPOSE

Engineer and inventor Bernard-Albin Gras, a lighting pioneer, created a revolutionary line of lamps that were admired by artists and designers from Henri Matisse to Le Corbusier to Coco Chanel.

A patent registered by Bernard-Albin Gras in 1921 marked the creation of the "Gras Adjustable Lamp"—and a revolution in task lighting. The product line that followed, including movable lamps, wall fixtures, and floor lamps, could be adapted to all kinds of working conditions, addressing the lighting needs of factories, offices, and many scientific professions. Gras lamps had a solution for every lighting challenge. They could be placed on or attached to a table, or hung from a wall or ceiling by a screw, clamp, or vise. With single or multiple ball-and-socket joints and adjustable shades, these task-based lamps were easy to use and comfortable for working and reading. In 1922, Bernard-Albin Gras sold his invention to the inventor Didier des Gachons. Working with his partner André-René Ravel, des Gachons broadened the collection and distributed it through an office equipment catalogue under the brand name Gras System R.A.V.E.L. Adjustable Lamp. An unprecedented combination of simplicity, ergonomics, durability, and functional aesthetics, these fixtures represent an important development in industrial design.

Gras adjustable lamps for a design table. On the left, model No. 211, enameled in black with three segments and a standard shade; on the right, model No. 204, with an elongated shade.

OPPOSITE
Demonstration plate, dated 1922, showing the principal models in the Gras collection.

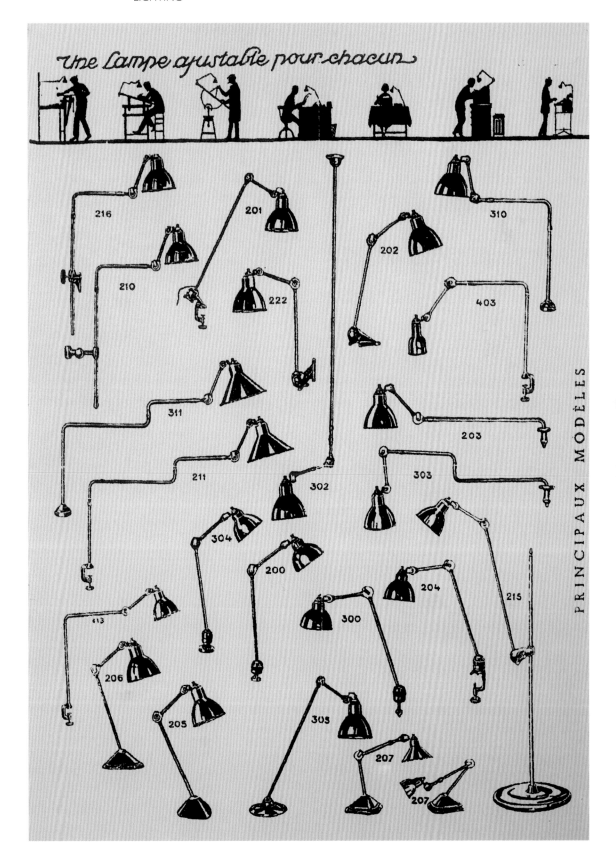

In an atelier restored by antiquarians Michel Peraches and Eric Miele, Gras floor and table lamps stand with a classic crystal chandelier and chairs, left to right, by Harry Bertoia, Mies van der Rohe, and Charles and Ray Eames.

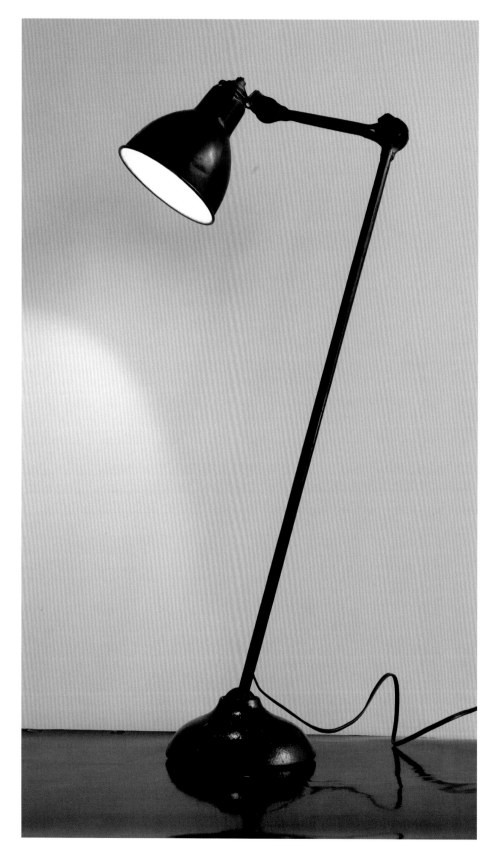

FROM LEFT TO RIGHT, TOP TO BOTTOM
Gras No. 305 lamp designed for heavy industrial machine work stands on a drafting table.

The lamp's name was engraved on the hinge of the early models.

Detail of the ball-and-socket joint mounted in the cast-metal base, as shown in Fig. 2 of the patent application (opposite).

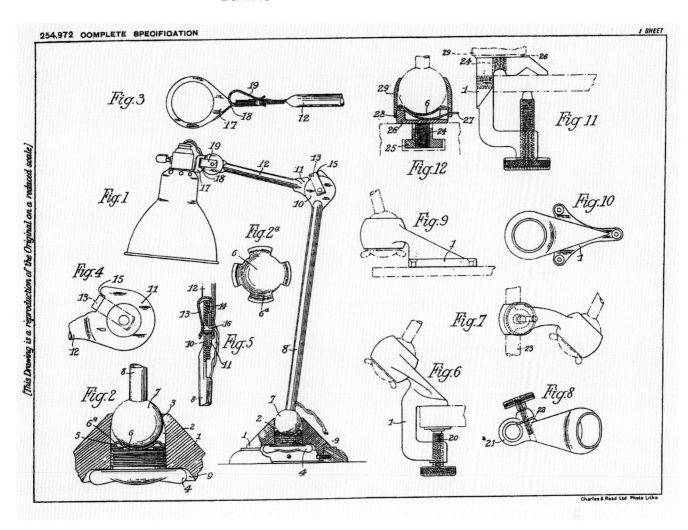

254,972 COMPLETE SPECIFICATION — 1 SHEET

[This Drawing is a reproduction of the Original on a reduced scale.]

SIMPLICITY AND HARMONY

Bernard-Albin Gras's adjustable lamps are designs that reflect the innovative spirit of this transformational period.

Simplicity and functionality were the goals of design in this new, industrial age. Le Corbusier admired the Gras lamp's sense of modernity; he used them to equip his architect's table and many of his design schemes, including the Pavillon Suisse in the Cité Internationale Universitaire in Paris. Numerous decorators and artists also contributed to the success of this celebrated work accessory: Robert Mallet-Stevens, Michel Roux-Spitz, Émil-Jacques Ruhlmann, René Herbst, Henri Matisse, Georges Braque, and Coco Chanel all lit their drafting tables and ateliers with Gras fixtures. This century-old collection has recently been reissued by the French company DCW. Its aesthetic, ergonomics, and simplicity still harmonize with contemporary interiors.

Plate of designs submitted in the United Kingdom by Didier des Gachons in 1921.

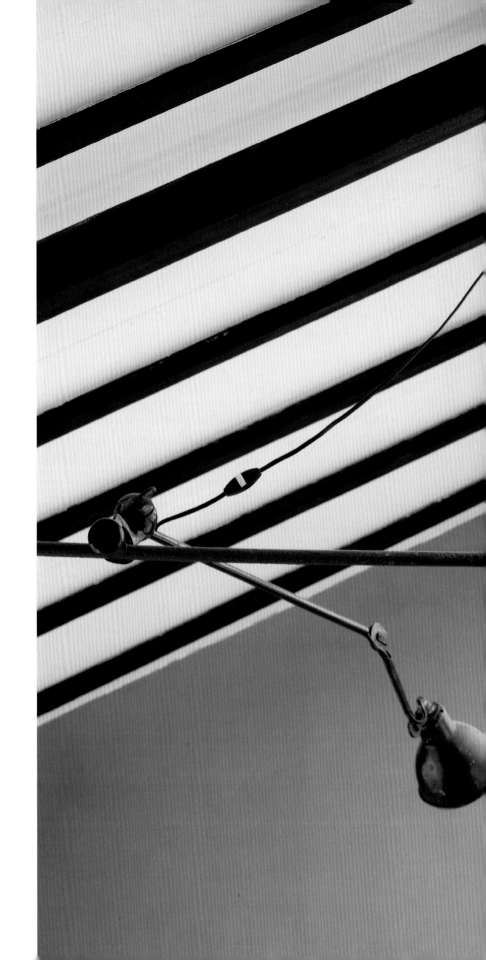

Beneath the skylight of a Paris apartment,
the long arms of several Gras lamp model
No. 201s are attached to a metal superstructure.

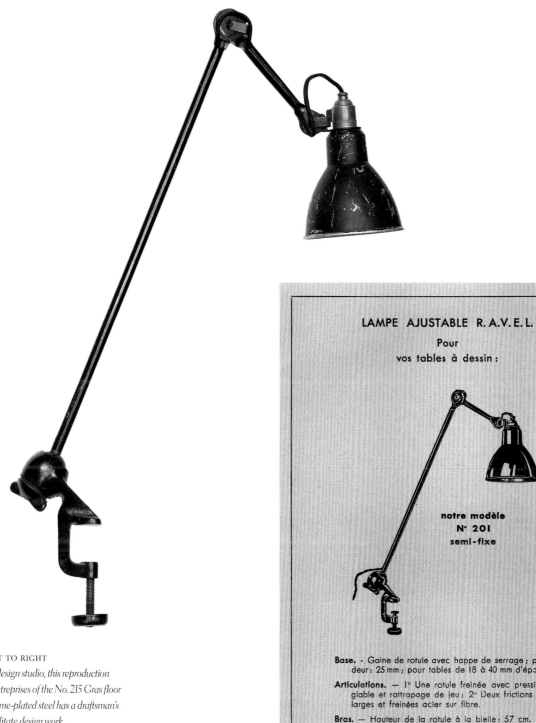

FROM LEFT TO RIGHT

Shown in a design studio, this reproduction by DCW Entreprises of the No. 215 Gras floor lamp in chrome-plated steel has a draftsman's shade to facilitate design work.

Distributed under R.A.V.E.L. starting in 1927, model No. 201 can be attached to a table. It is shown here, unrestored, in its original finish.

A page from the R.A.V.E.L. sales catalogue with technical specifications on model No. 201.

LAMPE AJUSTABLE R.A.V.E.L.

Pour
vos tables à dessin :

**notre modèle
N° 201
semi-fixe**

Base. - Gaine de rotule avec happe de serrage ; profondeur : 25 mm ; pour tables de 18 à 40 mm d'épaisseur.

Articulations. — 1° Une rotule freinée avec pression réglable et rattrapage de jeu ; 2° Deux frictions plates, larges et freinées acier sur fibre.

Bras. — Hauteur de la rotule à la bielle : 57 cm.

Bielle. - Longueur d'axe en axe : 16 cm.

Collier à douille porte-réflecteur. — Trou de 28 mm ; distance de son point d'articulation au centre du trou : 50 mm.

Réflecteur normal N° 1054. — Hauteur : 140 mm ; diamètre : 130 mm.

Décor. — Emaillé noir, nickelé, oxydé ou chromé.

5

This collector's piece, on display in the Galerie
Anne-Sophie Duval in Paris, is a very personal
interpretation of the Gras lamp by Eileen Gray.
The designer set the model No. 222 on a base
of sanded Oregon pine.

OPPOSITE
This rare lamp, known as the 360, displayed
in the Galerie Duo, was designed by René Herbst.
It can turn all the way around on its axis.

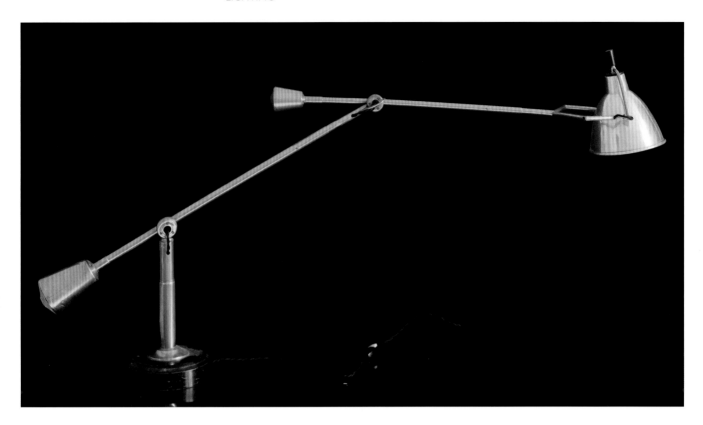

FUNCTIONAL BEAUTY

Édouard-Wilfrid Buquet's "seesaw" lamp is considered to be the perfect balance of aesthetics and functionality.

In 1923 in Paris, Édouard-Wilfrid Buquet registered a patent in the Machine category that described the invention of a balancing support for lighting apparatuses. The device was a very sophisticated system of levers, joints, and counterweights that allowed for mathematically precise balance. This invention, which essentially acted as a lever, could be applied to the design of a lamp to minimize the exertion of directing its beam and to ensure the stability of its support.

Five years later, Buquet registered a patent that specified the practical use of his invention, the "Lampe Equilibrée," which he called a "lighting fixture that can be directed with articulated arms." Capable of directing and concentrating a light source with a touch of a hand, it was intended for workers as varied as architects, designers, photographers, artisans, and dentists. The lamp would always keep its balance: its center of gravity and the existence of the counterweight ensured complete stability in all positions, and each arm could be directed independently. Advertisements boasted that the Lampe Equilibrée provided the answers to every need.

Architects Le Corbusier and Charlotte Perriand used the lamp in their installations, including the 1929 Autumn Salon in Paris. The elegant style of Buquet's design appealed to the decorator Émil-Jacques Ruhlmann, who used it to furnish his own offices. This legendary lamp is still being produced and remains an exemplary combination of ingenious design and aesthetics. It is of no surprise that it is included in the Museum of Modern Art's collection.

FROM LEFT TO RIGHT
Aluminum shade of a Buquet lamp, equipped with a Bakelite handle to direct the light source.

Now reissued by Tecnolumen, the Type A lamp with a wide range of movement is intended for architects, engineers, and designers. The base is lacquered wood, and the nickel-plated arms have lead counterweights. Tecnolumen has reissued the complete Buquet lamp collection.

THE HISTORY OF A PROTOTYPE

The highly influential articulated Anglepoise lamp was a by-product of a curious engineer's experiments.

George Carwardine, a British engineer who specialized in suspension systems for the automobile industry, liked to experiment. While tinkering in his workshop in Bath, he managed to create a new type of spring that was flexible yet would remain in place after being moved in every direction; all he had to do next was invent something that would put his discovery to use. He eventually designed a lamp that could illuminate not only specific parts of suspension systems for his workers but also the documents and books on his worktable. Just as constant tension between the muscles is needed to balance and stabilize the human arm, a combination of Carwardine's springs maintained the lamp's balance and allowed its articulated sections—corresponding to the wrist, elbow, and shoulder— to be locked into any position desired. The twentieth century's first articulated lamp combined a stable base, a focused beam, and great flexibility for a broad scope of work.

The first articulated lamp, the Anglepoise, designed in 1931 by George Carwardine, was inspired by the functioning of the human arm.

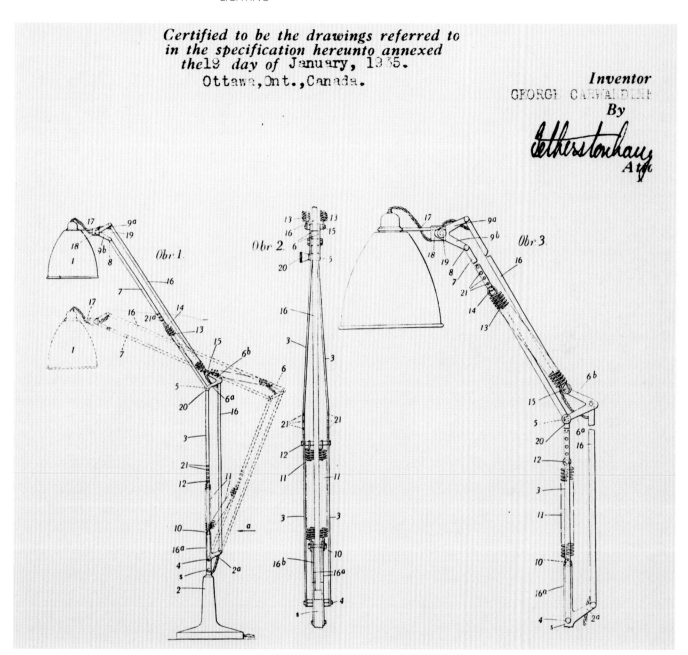

Certified to be the drawings referred to in the specification hereunto annexed the 19 day of January, 1935.
Ottawa, Ont., Canada.

Inventor
GEORGE CARWARDINE
By
Fetherstonhaugh
Atty

In 1932, George Carwardine registered an initial patent, and a few years later he entered into a partnership with the industrialist Herbert Terry to produce and market this new lamp. They had hoped to name it "Equipoise," but since this name was already registered, the lamp was baptized "Anglepoise," suggesting its adaptability. The original version had four springs. The inventor and the team from Herbert Terry & Sons perfected a new model for domestic use—the timeless Anglepoise 1227. The Terry firm, established in 1855, has been managed by the same family for six generations. In 2009, the original 1227 was reissued to celebrate the seventy-fifth anniversary of the Anglepoise lamp. An innovative design that functions flawlessly, George Carwardine's articulated lamp brilliantly illustrates the innovative spirit of the Machine Age. The 1227 remains a model of creativity and is still the task lamp par excellence.

Page from a patent for an invention registered by George Carwardine in 1935.

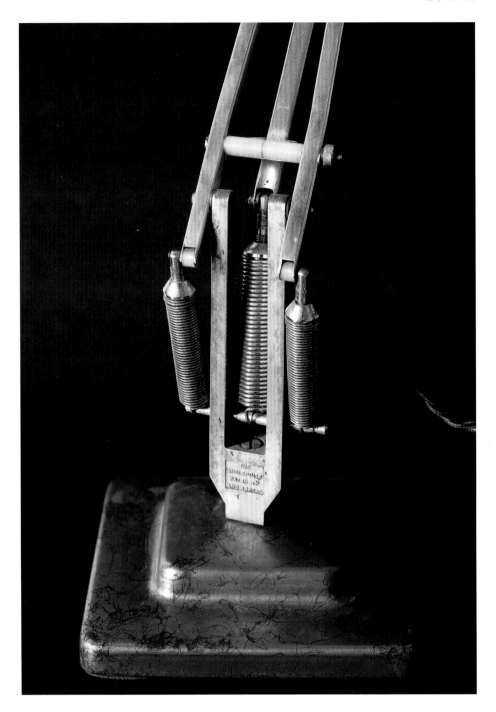

The Anglepoise spring system provided flexibility yet allowed the light to be fixed in position as it was adjusted. The logo engraved on the shaft reads, "The Anglepoise."

OPPOSITE
Originally designed for industrial purposes, the three-spring Anglepoise 1227 was adopted for domestic use.

OVERLEAF
In an antique dealer's atelier, the Jieldé Standard lamp attached to a workbench occupies the location it was designed for and performs its original function.

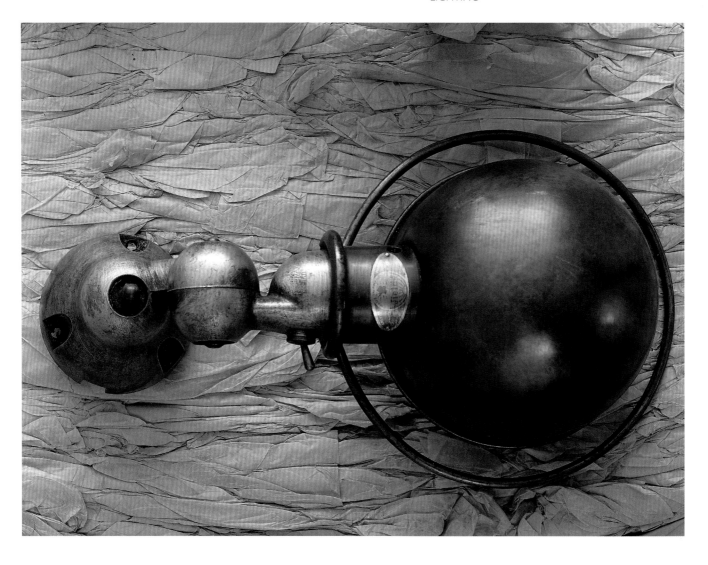

THE IDEAL LAMP

Indestructible, indefatigable, and watertight, the Jieldé Standard light was widely considered to be the ideal work lamp.

This lamp is revolutionary in its conception. With no cord, it receives electrical current via articulated copper connectors. The Jieldé can safely rotate 360 degrees and be modified using four standardized, interchangeable elements. Any positioning is possible: the lamp can be stretched out flat or shortened according to the requirements of the task at hand. Remarkably stable, it is attached to the worktable with a sturdy clamp device, and a metal ring encircling the edge of the shade makes it easy to direct the light. Industrial companies found it to be the ideal work lamp and ordered it in large quantities. Inspired by its success, its inventor, Lyonnais engineer Jean Louis Domecq, started the Jieldé firm in 1953, using the phonetic rendering of his own initials for its name. A fixture originally designed for Domecq's own atelier and produced for industrial workshops, the Standard can now be found in offices and design studios. The lamp is still being produced in Lyon today, and its many virtues ensure its continuing popularity.

A technical and functional innovation, the cordless Jieldé Standard lamp is distinguished by a metal ring around the shade to make it easy to direct the light. It bears a riveted label with the map of France.

OPPOSITE
Resting on a packing table, Jieldé floor lamps are ready to begin a new life in Japan.

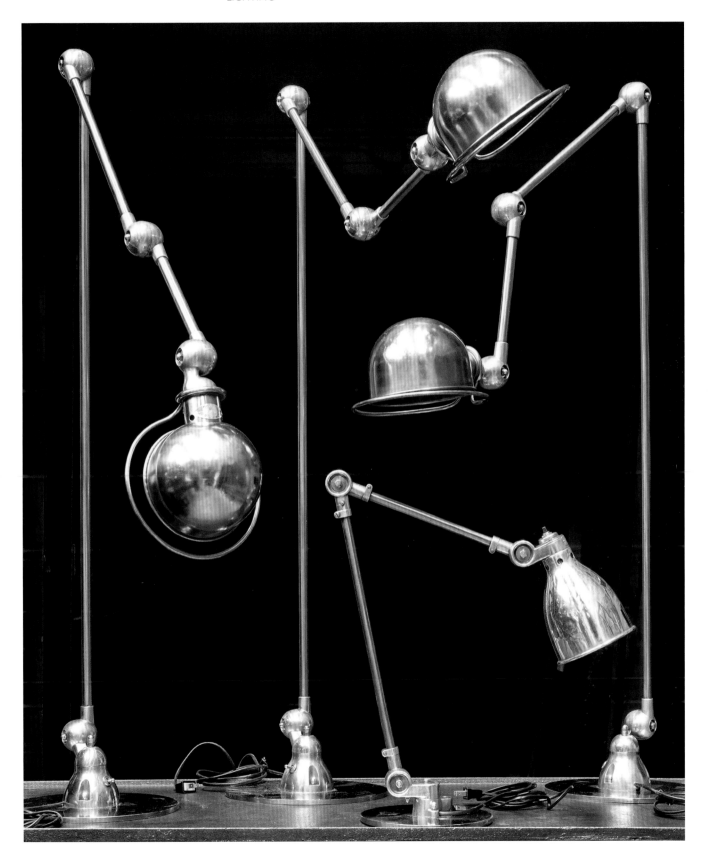

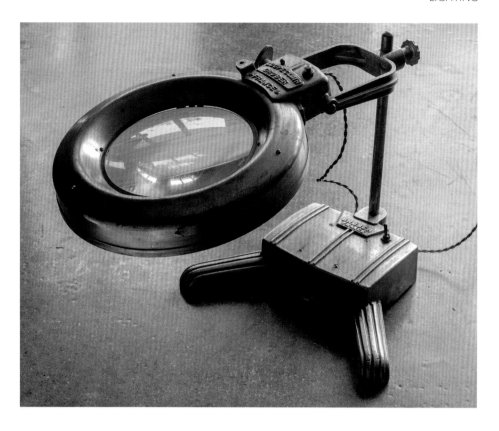

Dissolving Shadows: Scientific Lighting

Adapting lighting to the rigors of the medical professions required significant innovations.

The first and most brilliant of these innovations came from Louis-François Verain, a surgeon and engineer at the medical school of Algiers. In 1919, he registered a patent in Paris for an invention that provided bright light and eliminated cast shadows, perfect for surgeons or designers. A combination of optical components and a conical mirror directed intense light uniformly over a work area. Scialytic (from the Greek, meaning "to dissolve shadows") lamps were produced and distributed by the company Barbier, Benard & Turenne (often abbreviated as BBT). This revolutionary light has made a major contribution to medical progress—so much so that its name has since become the generic term for surgical lighting.

FROM LEFT TO RIGHT

Gruber's Loupeclaire combines an intense light source and magnification, ideal for the precise work of watchmakers and jewelers.

The Scialytic operating room light produced by BBT eliminates cast shadows.

Drawing with Light: Artistic Lighting

Advancements in projecting and reflecting light fostered a new art form, photography, a word that derives from the Greek photos *and* graphos *meaning "drawing with light."*

At the end of the nineteenth century, the photographer Nadar began to experiment with new techniques. He was the first to use artificial light when he embarked on photographing the catacombs beneath the streets of Paris. The emergence of this new profession soon resulted in a proliferation of photographic studios, with the proprietors exploring the range of the medium by experimenting with lighting. Natural light provided soft, low-contrast illumination, but a camera required long exposures to capture an image. The development and refinement of reflectors and shades allowed photographers to focus and adjust the quantity of light on a subject, enabling them to control exposure times and truly "draw with light."

Kodasol projector lamp with diffuse light intended for use in photography studios.

OPPOSITE
Lita projector lamps with adjustable heights on display at Objets en Transit in Paris.

OVERLEAF
The shade for the Ascialux light made by Société GAL measured 30 inches (75 centimeters) in diameter. Intended for sports centers and classrooms, and offered in an array of colors, these fixtures in vivid hues are valued by collectors. As their catalogue proclaimed, they provide "exceptional visual comfort."

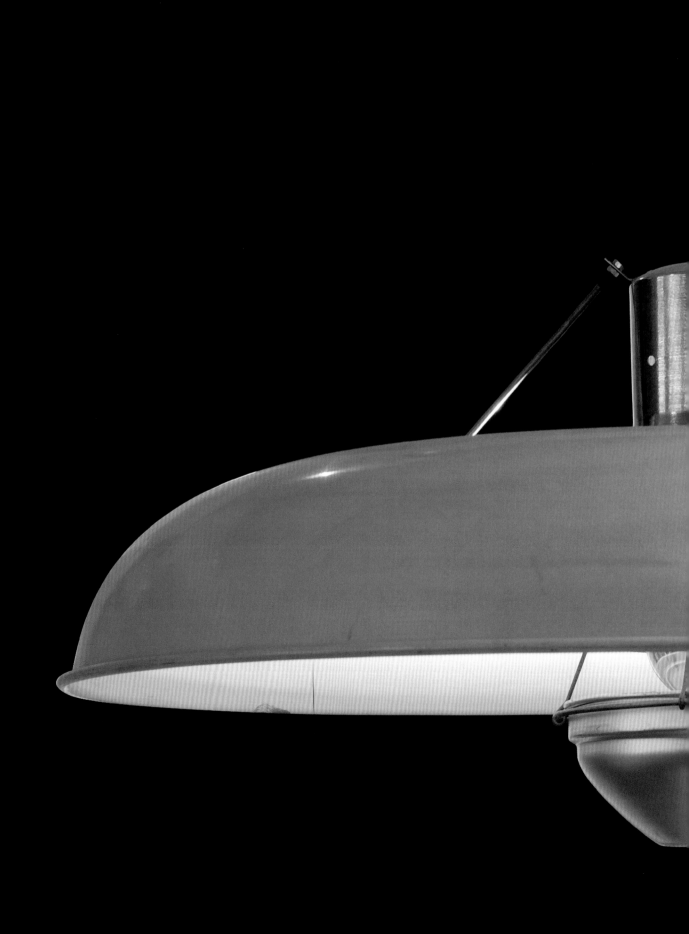

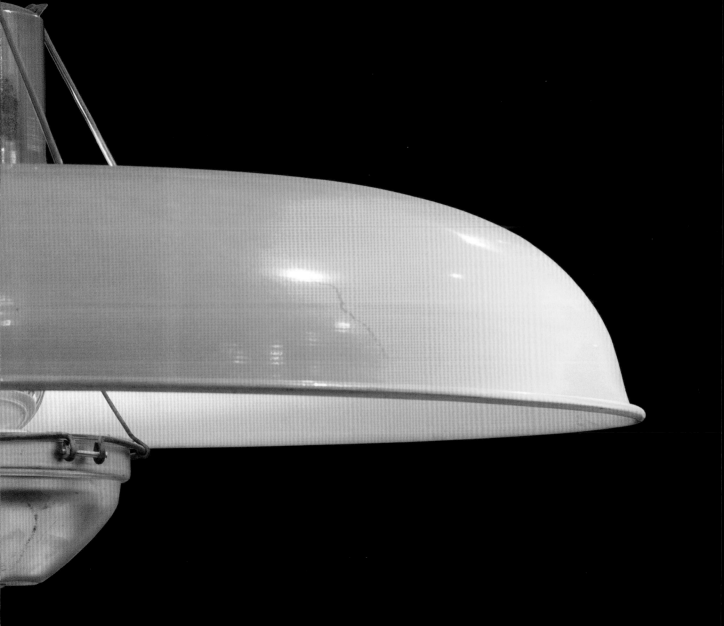

Factory lamps attached to the frame of
an industrial antiques stand at the Saint-Ouen
flea market in Paris.

OPPOSITE
High-powered Brandt projector lamps were
sturdy and effective fixtures for railway stations,
warehouses, and public spaces.

FORM AND FUNCTION: INDUSTRIAL LIGHTING

*Factories were no longer built on a human scale in the early twentieth century; lighting these immense
spaces required powerful, specialized fixtures.*

Workplaces that had previously functioned on a human scale were replaced by vast
installations built to accommodate heavy machinery and store large quantities of material
and merchandise. A new form of industrial architecture appeared, utilizing concrete
and metal. Densely populated with employees producing at high rates of speed and intense
levels of precision, every part of these enormous factories needed to be lit. Lighting these
immense manufacturing spaces and public facilities required a broad range of specialized,
powerful fixtures.

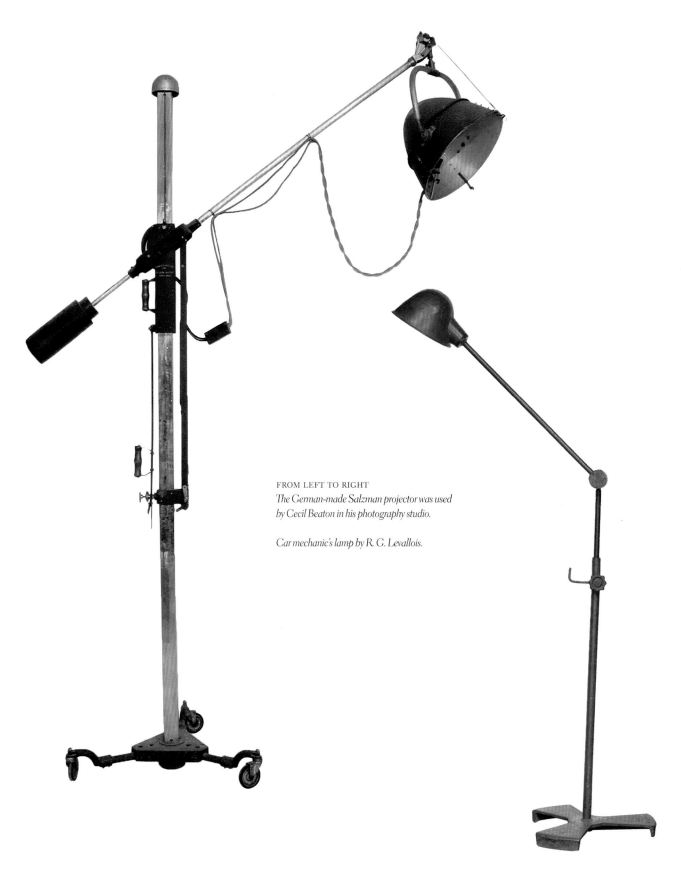

FROM LEFT TO RIGHT

The German-made Salzman projector was used
by Cecil Beaton in his photography studio.

Car mechanic's lamp by R. G. Levallois.

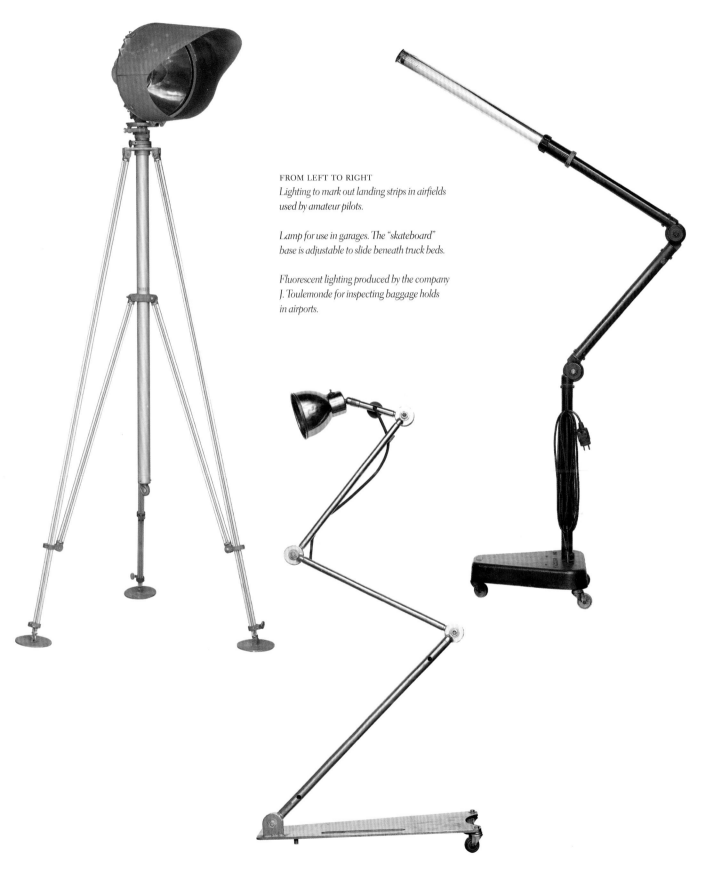

FROM LEFT TO RIGHT
*Lighting to mark out landing strips in airfields
used by amateur pilots.*

*Lamp for use in garages. The "skateboard"
base is adjustable to slide beneath truck beds.*

*Fluorescent lighting produced by the company
J. Toulemonde for inspecting baggage holds
in airports.*

*A variety of industrial lamp models marked
with their brand logos: Philips, Mazda, LG,
and Reflecto-Luxelles. Each has its own
distinctive personality. Now restored to their
original condition, their streamlined shapes
are again part of everyday life in both public
and domestic spaces.*

OVERLEAF
*Before restoration in an antiquarian's atelier,
industrial lamps of gray- and khaki-painted
sheet metal hang thickly coated with dust.*

CURIOSITIES

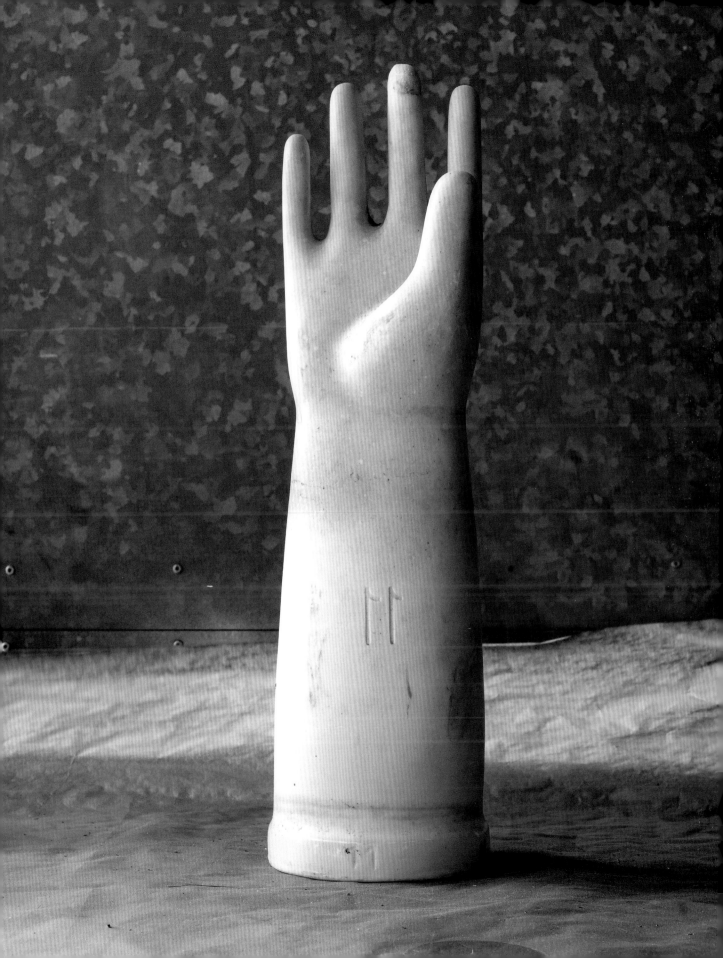

INDUSTRIAL NOSTALGIA

The transition from artisanal craftsmanship to industrial production was accompanied by the design of utilitarian objects that can now be viewed as objets d'art in their own right.

Whether an integral part of the production chain or reserved for a more narrowly defined purpose, factory equipment was above all practical and effective. Devices were carefully crafted to simplify work, speed production, and guarantee the consistent quality of a finished product.

Electric clocks were prominently displayed in all public spaces and factories to coordinate activities and schedules. Their widespread presence facilitated the management of work carried out by teams, which increasingly replaced the craftsmanship of individual artisans alone at their tasks. Timepieces set the pace of the workday, commuting schedules, and everyday life.

Innovations in equipment and materials, a growing demand for comfort and modernity, and the broadening product range available combined to boost the allure of an updated pastime: shopping. The consumer became a force that generated the creation of publicity items enthusiastically promoting brand names. Merchants and artisans publicized themselves and their wares with signs and billboards composed of gigantic, colorful lettering. Commercial art flourished.

Today, these objects are appealing mementos of a pioneering era. Sometimes they no longer have a functional purpose, their forms seeming odd and whimsical to our eyes. Yet, as invaluable witnesses to twentieth-century progress, they are much admired and sought after by contemporary collectors to fill their own cabinets of curiosities.

Clocks no longer in use await restoration in an antique dealer's atelier.

PAGE 175
Porcelain mold used for making rubber gloves.

TIMEKEEPERS

When electricity began to power clocks, timepieces took on a greater role of synchronizing commerce and society.

Electric clocks set the pace for the intense activity of industrialization. But public timepieces that synchronized communities were in use in France as early as 1740, when the royal master watchmaker and founder of the Lepaute clockmaking firm was charged with the responsibility of constructing large timepieces for public use. To this day, Lepaute clocks adorn the facades of great Parisian buildings such as the Louvre and the Palais Royal. In 1933, they installed a luminous clock 65 feet (20 meters) in diameter on the Eiffel Tower; it was commissioned by an industrialist for publicity. Synchronized clocks were installed in schools and workplaces, using a central master clock that regulated a group of secondary clocks. These ensured that everyone, from student to worker, kept on schedule. Built to last, public clocks—with faces and gears that are of monumental size or sleekly efficient industrial models—still keep time in ateliers and lofts.

Two restored cast-aluminum centrally controlled secondary clocks, signed by Brillié and Lepaute, built for railway stations, administrative offices, and public spaces. They now hold a place of honor in a branch office and the brasserie L'Institut in Paris.

OVERLEAF
An array of restored clocks representing Brillié, Ato, and Delambre brands.

The central clock that synchronized as many as twelve secondary clocks.

OPPOSITE
Still in working condition in a private home, this clock's gold-leafed and metal face measures almost 5 feet (1½ meters) in diameter.

A remarkable invention by the engineer Lucien Brillié, a synchronization system allowed several clocks to be regulated by a central control. Restored from their abandoned and dilapidated state by contemporary dealers, these clocks recover their original roles as timekeepers as they pass through the attentive hands of restoration experts.

SCIENTIFIC GLASSWARE

Tools of the chemical and medical industries were refined, creating beautiful, utilitarian objects.

The early twentieth century was an extraordinarily fruitful period of scientific discovery. Schools specialized in teaching the sciences were equipped like professional medical laboratories with measuring devices, test tubes, and flasks. No longer used for their original purpose, this medical glassware is sought after by today's collectors.

184

Collection of laboratory glassware displayed at Ghislain Antiques at the Saint-Ouen flea market in Paris.

VESTIGES OF THE NINETEENTH CENTURY

The modern era was marked by the use of steel, heavy machinery, and mass production,
but the spirit of the nineteenth century lived on in traditional craftsmanship.

The development of commerce, progress in the sciences, and expansion of the railway
network accelerated business activity at the beginning of the twentieth century. Specially
designed objects that met the specific requirements of a profession or function may have
been produced with modern techniques, but they were carefully fabricated with attention
to detail. For example, medical cabinets used by doctors and dentists were designed
so that their medicine and instruments were not easily accessible to all. The importance
of their aesthetic appeal is also evident.

Pharmacists' containers, used to protect
medicine ingredients from exposure to light.

OPPOSITE
Bottle from a school laboratory in Neuilly.

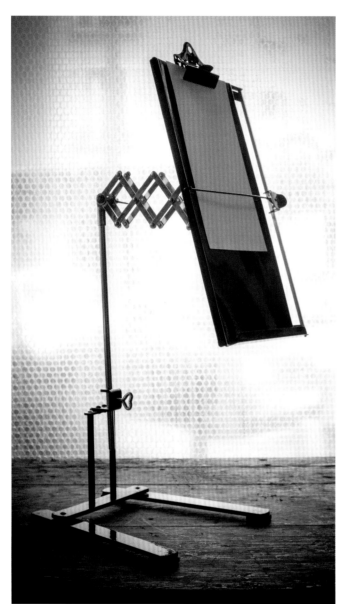

USEFUL OBJECTS

Carefully designed accessories made workers more comfortable and ensured the quality of their work.

Office and workshop accessories provided solutions for very specific functions and practical ways of executing tasks. They included special lighting devices for railway workers on the track network and office accessories to help with typing. These reliable, familiar tools were always within arm's reach.

FROM LEFT TO RIGHT

Paper holder to assist typists. The support is extendable and adjustable in height; a horizontal guide shows how far the work has progressed.

Electric cast-aluminum lamp used for railway track inspections, with BBT logo, c. 1930.

Cast-metal shoemaker's organizer. The rotating trays held the many types of nails required for his work.

Copper and cast-iron fan from the early twentieth century.

OPPOSITE
Stacked military campaign trunks made from stamped-iron sheet metal with bronze locks.

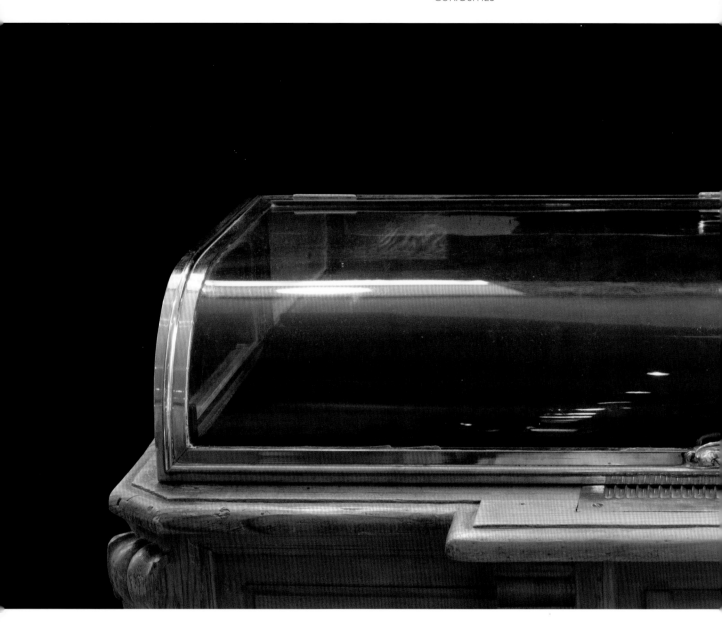

WOODEN DESIGNS

Wooden furniture was often replaced in factories by sturdier metal pieces, yet wood remained popular in more traditional establishments.

Wood, a traditional, timeless material, was used in sewing ateliers and small textile production facilities. Wooden counters, display cases, and shelving were often paired with glass and metal trim, the warmth of wood and the cool industrial quality of the metal and glass complementing each other. Some of these fixtures are still preserved in shops that treasure this evocative furniture from a bygone era.

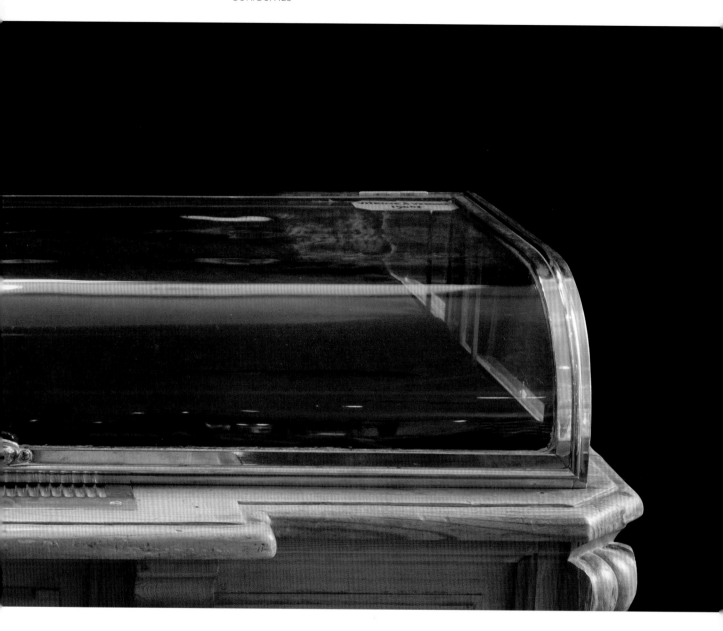

A storefront window made of bombé copper and glass now used as a display case for fashion accessories at A la Bonne Renommée in the Marais district of Paris.

An impressive wooden chest from a button-making factory. Every one of its 120 drawers is fitted with a label holder. A rare collection of Gras lamps stand on top of the chest.

MASS PRODUCTION

The stamps and molds designed to manufacture workaday objects are themselves objects of beauty.

Twentieth-century production employed techniques that were far removed from those of traditional artisanal craftsmanship. Fabrication evolved from producing handcrafted, singular pieces to large-scale, fast-paced, high-volume production of multiple units. Powerful machines were designed to manufacture metal objects by essentially stamping, or compressing, metal sheeting between a concave mold and a relief form. Other, more flexible working materials, such as rubber, could be molded by using a soaking process for industrial fabrication.

Dies for fabricating decorated buttons customized with the emblem of a club or a profession.

OPPOSITE
Porcelain molds for fabricating rubber gloves from Ets Coquet, a porcelain manufacturer whose workers needed to use gloves with nonslip textured surfaces.

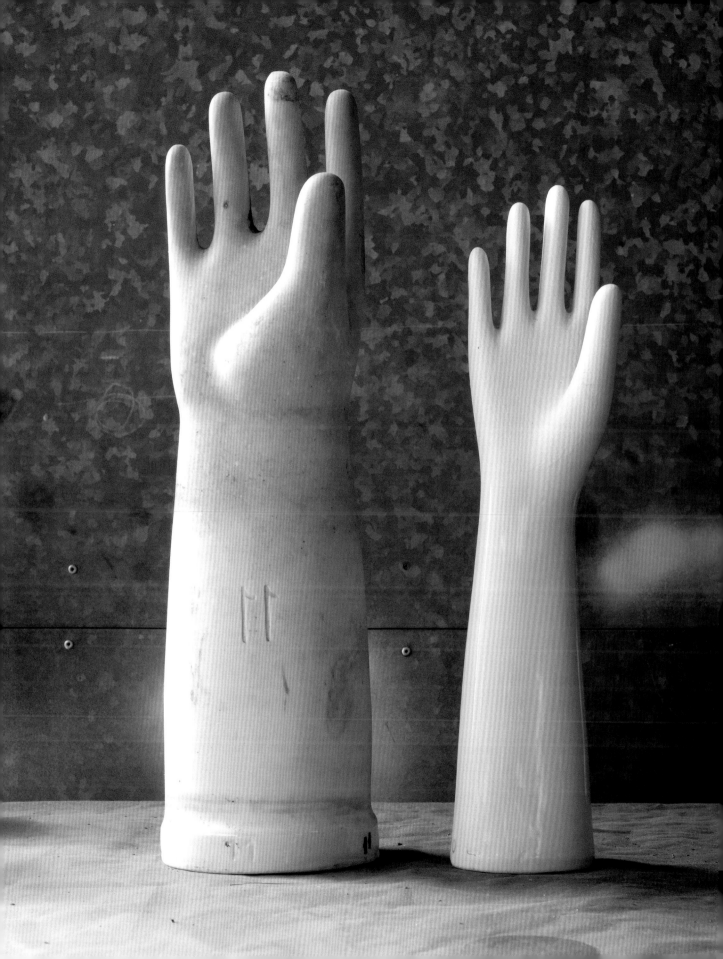

Cast metal dies used for producing ornaments.
A sheet of metal was compressed between
a relief form and a mold to form the article.

OPPOSITE
One of the steel dies used in hat making. A sheet
of moistened felt was inserted and compressed
between the two forms.

LIGHTING AND COMMERCE

Shoppers flocked to city sidewalks and department stores, while proprietors illuminated their wares invitingly.

Bright public lighting and illumination from shop windows added to the pleasure of the archetypal modern pastime: shopping. As fast as industrialization could place new, reasonably priced products on the store shelves, consumers spent money to purchase them. Department stores, which had first appeared in the nineteenth century, flourished; their modern glass and metal architecture elevated them to symbolic cathedrals of commerce. Elevators and pedestrian bridges were designed to allow patrons to move about freely as they admired brightly illuminated shelves of merchandise. Not just shoppers crowded department stores; those eager "to see and be seen" joined the daily promenade through these inviting spaces.

Urban streetlight measuring 18 inches (45 centimeters) in diameter, made of molded glass and bearing the Holophane logo. It was designed for illuminating broad, open spaces like squares, avenues, and sidewalks.

OPPOSITE
Reflectors for illuminating shop display cases in silver gilt glass.

The Art of Publicity

Faced with an abundance and diversity of choices, consumers often chose products that were promoted with vivid colors and evocative images.

Posters, signs, and catalogues were the tools of promotion. The graphic arts flourished in these years, and well-known artists, including Toulouse-Lautrec, willingly participated in developing brand images. Merchants featured their wares in elegant, flattering displays in shop windows and interiors. The atmosphere of street life was changed by luminous signs and attractive arrangements of merchandise in window displays. A number of these curious objects, rescued from oblivion, are popular items in antiques shops.

FROM LEFT TO RIGHT, TOP TO BOTTOM
Chest belonging to a paint seller. Painted circles on the drawers show the many colors available.

The cover of a Strafor catalogue features a figure in the dynamic graphic style of the 1920s.

Metal plaque identifying a Singer sewing machine. Letters are stamped in relief in zinc.

An enameled advertising plaque dated 1929, by the renowned artist Charles Loupot, whose advertising designs typified the Machine Age aesthetic.

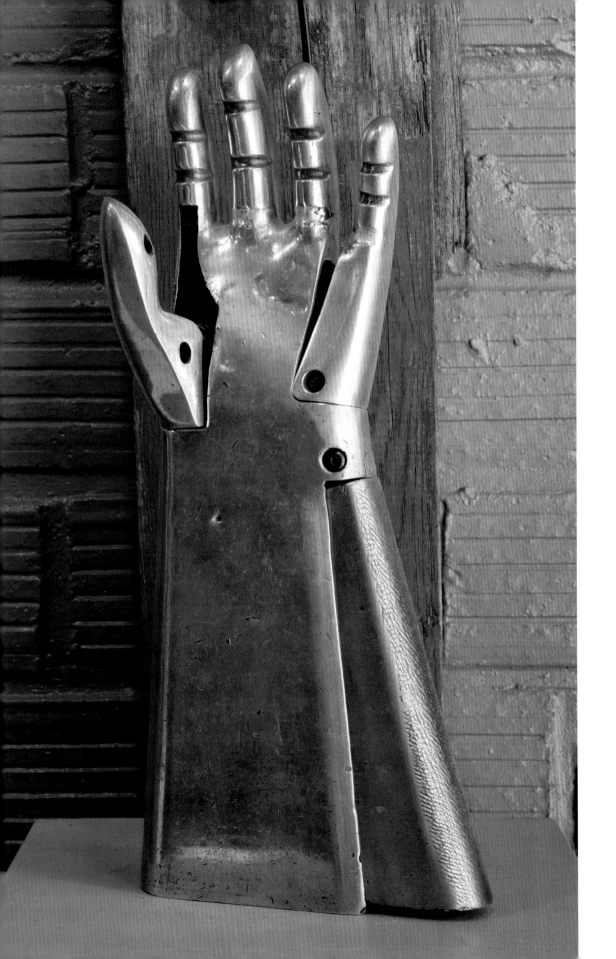

A giant articulated steel hand and a footprint displayed at Gilles Oudin at the Saint-Ouen flea market in Paris. These fantastical objects originally belonged to a glove seller.

THE PATINA OF AGE

Each layer of paint and every scrape and ding bears witness to a hardworking past.

As we observe the patina of time—those successive layers of paint and old inscriptions—it is easy to imagine the intimate relationship that once existed between these serviceable tools and their users. These reflections lend a personal quality to an otherwise utilitarian object. Such reminders bring us closer to the richly human aspects of industry.

Gras lamp painted by its user in a workshop's storage cabinet. The white traces on the wall mark the placement of old shelves that have since disappeared.

OPPOSITE
Tool cabinet of zinc sheet metal with a bluish-green patina from exposure to humidity next to an R. G. Levallois garage lamp in its original color.

FROM LEFT TO RIGHT, TOP TO BOTTOM
Chest of small drawers for sorting tools.

Office file cabinets with drop-down doors. Overlaid coats of paint suggest multiple owners over the years.

Office file cabinets with many successive layers of paint.

Molten metal was poured into these wooden molds to make pipes and hoses. In this factory, the colors had significance: red, black, and writing on the various molds informed the manufacture of parts of all sizes.

OPPOSITE
A whale bone placed on a casting mold in its original red finish styled by antique dealer Martine Valli.

Bronze lettering posed in the cubbyholes of a factory cabinet.

OPPOSITE
Made of frosted glass and metal, this giant, luminous letter was part of a shopping center sign from the 1950s.

WORDPLAY

Fragments of commercial or industrial parts used for advertising or manufacturing can create a dramatic effect.

Eye-catching billboards and signs on facades of businesses attracted the attention of passersby. The letters composing the signs were fashioned from painted sheet metal, precious metals, or wood, each material quite distinctive and evoking a message that the business wished to convey. Signs ranged from workmanlike to artful and were often on an exaggerated scale. Once these letters were illuminated, their visibility—and their message—reached even more people.

FROM LEFT TO RIGHT
A composition of letters arranged above a filing cabinet with drop-down doors and a Gras lamp at Atelier 154 in Paris.

An array of letters, some crude and some refined.

OVERLEAF
A stylishly lettered message on the walls of a shop that features industrial antiques in the Marais neighborhood of Paris.

RESOURCES

PARIS

ATELIER 154
14/16 rue Neuve Popincourt
75011 Paris
+33 6 62 32 79 06
www.atelier154.com

GALERIE ANNE-SOPHIE DUVAL
5 Quai Malaquais
75006 Paris
+ 33 1 43 54 51 16
galerie@annesophieduval.com

GALERIE DUO
15 rue de Lille
75007 Paris
+33 1 47 03 92 63
duocardinael@wanadoo.fr

JOUSSE ENTERPRISE
18 rue de Seine
75006 Paris
+33 1 53 82 13 60
infos@jousse-entreprise.com

JÉRÔME LEPERT
106 rue Vieille du Temple
75003 Paris
+33 6 10 18 18 88
lepert.jerome@wanadoo.fr

LES NOUVEAUX BROCANTEURS
935 rue de Paris
60520 La Chapelle en Serval
+33 6 62 75 64 85
www.lesnouveauxbrocanteurs.com

MERCI
111 boulevard Beaumarchais
75003 Paris
+33 1 42 77 00 33
www.merci-merci.com

JEAN-CHARLES RIBES
20 rue Caulaincourt
75018 Paris
+33 1 42 58 35 28
www.design-antiquites.fr

ZUT!
9 rue de Ravignan
75018 Paris
+ 33 1 42 59 69 68
www.antiquites-industrielles.com

Shops and stands at the Saint-Ouen flea market

GHISLAIN ANTIQUES
97 rue des Rosiers
www.ghislainantiques.com

OBJETS EN TRANSIT
Marché Dauphine, stand 122
www.objetsentransit.com

GILLES OUDIN
Marché Paul Bert, allée 7, stand 405
+33 06 10 20 53 26
www.bravard-oudin.fr

MICHEL PERACHES–ERIC MIELE
Marché Paul Bert, allée 1, stand 21
peraches.miele@gmail.com

QUINTESSENCE
14 rue Paul Bert
www.quintessenceplayground.com

VALLI
Marché Paul Bert, allée 3, stand 159
martinevalli@noos.fr

VANITY LIFESTYLE
3 rue Paul Bert
+33 6 13 59 93 88
www.vanitylifestyle.fr

LONDON

ALFIE'S ANTIQUE MARKET
13–25 Church Street
Marylebone
London NW8 8DT
www.alfiesantiques.com

ANDREW NEBBETT ANTIQUES
35–37 Church Street Marylebone
London NW8 8ES
+44 207 723 2303
www.andrewnebbett.com

BRICK LANE MARKET
Brick Lane, Shoreditch
London E1 6PU
www.visitbricklane.org

ELEMENTAL
130 Shoreditch High Street
London E1 6JE
www.elemental.uk.com

ENCORE RECLAMATION
The Old Spratts Factory
Unit 4 Block B, 2 Fawe Street
London E14 6PD
By appointment only
+44 207 001 7605
www.encorereclamation.co.uk

LASSCO BRUNSWICK HOUSE
30 Wandsworth Road
Vauxhall, London E1 6PU
www.lassco.co.uk

OLD SPITALFIELDS MARKET
16 Horner Square, Spitalfields
London E1 6EW
www.oldspitalfieldsmarket.com

LITTLE PARIS
39 Park Road
London N8 8TE
+44 208 340 9008

262 Upper Street
London N1 2UQ
+44 207 704 9970
www.littleparis.co.uk

PORTOBELLO MARKET
Portobello Road
London W10 5TD
www.portobelloroad.co.uk

RETROUVIUS
1016 Harrow Road
Kensal Green
London NW10 5NS
+44 208 960 6060
www.retrouvius.com

THE CONRAN SHOP
Michelin House
81 Fulham Road
London SW3 6RD
+44 207 589 7401

55 Marylebone High Street
London W1U 5HS
+44 207 723 2223
www.conranshop.co.uk

THE OLD CINEMA
160 Chiswick High Road
London W4 1PR
+44 208 995 4166
www.theoldcinema.co.uk

WILLESDEN SALVAGE
189 High Road, Willesden
London NW10 2SD
+44 208 459 2947
www.willesdensalvage.co.uk

NEW YORK

1STDIBS
156 5th Avenue, Suite 200
New York, NY 10010
www.1stdibs.com

ABC CARPET & HOME
888 Broadway
New York, NY 10003
212 473 3000
www.abchome.com

CITY FOUNDRY
365 Atlantic Avenue
Brooklyn, NY 11217
718 923 1786
www.cityfoundry.com

CRATE & BARREL
611 Broadway
New York, NY 10012
212 780 0004

650 Madison Avenue
New York, NY 10022
212 308 0011
www.crateandbarrel.com

DESIGN WITHIN REACH
110 Greene Street
New York, NY 10012
212 475 0001

341 Columbus Avenue
New York, NY 10024
212 799 5900

957 3rd Avenue
New York, NY 10022
212 888 4539

903 Broadway
New York, NY 10010
212 477 1155
www.dwr.com

HELL'S KITCHEN FLEA MARKET
West 39th Street and 9th Avenue
New York, NY 10018
www.hellskitchenfleamarket.com

HOLLER & SQUALL
119 Atlantic Avenue
Brooklyn, NY 11201
347 405 3734
www.hollerandsquall.com

LOST CITY ARTS
18 Cooper Square
New York, NY 10003
212 375 0500
www.lostcityarts.com

OLDE GOOD THINGS
149 Madison Avenue
New York, NY 10016
212 321 0770

302 Bowery
New York, NY 10012
212 498 9922

450 Columbus Avenue
New York, NY 10024
212 362 8025

5 East 16th Street
New York, NY 10003
212 989 8814

124 West 24th Street
New York, NY 10011
212 989 8401
www.ogtstore.com

PAULA RUBENSTEIN LTD
21 Bond Street
New York, NY 10012
212 966 8954

RePOP
143 Roebling Street
Brooklyn, NY 11211
718 260 8032

68 Washington Avenue
Brooklyn, NY 11205
718 260 8032
www.repopny.com

Restoration Hardware
935 Broadway
New York, NY 10010
212 260 9479
www.restorationhardware.com

Two Jakes
320 Wythe Avenue
Brooklyn, NY 11249
718 782 7780
www.twojakes.com

Urban Archeology
143 Franklin Street
New York, NY 10013
212 431 4646
NYdowntown@urbanarchaeology.com

239 East 58th Street
New York, NY 10022
212 371 4646
NYuptown@urbanarchaeology.com

2231 Montauk Highway
Bridgehampton, NY 11932
631 537 0124
bridgehampton@urbanarchaeology.com

WRK Design
32 Prince Street
New York, NY 10012
212 947 2281
www.wrkdesign.com

Wyeth
315 Spring Street
New York, NY 10013
212 243 3661
www.wyethome.com

Distributors

Anglepoise, Ltd.
Unit A10 Railway Triangle, Walton Road,
Farlington PO6 ITN, Great Britain
+44 2 392 224 450
www.anglepoise.com

Ciguë (Mullca chair)
www.cigue.net
furniture@cigue.net

DCW Entreprises
(Gras lamp and Surpil chair)
71 rue de la Fontaine au Roi
75011 Paris, France
+33 1 40 21 37 60
www.lampegras.com
www.surpil.com

Emeco (Navy chair)
805 Elm Avenue
Hannover, PA 17331 USA
800 366 5951
Int. +1 717 637 5951
www.emeco.net

Holophane
3825 Columbus Road SW
Granville, OH 43023 USA
866 465 6742
www.holophane.com

Jieldé
9 rue du Dauphiné
69800 Saint-Priest, France
+33 4 78 20 10 16
www.jielde.com

Société MIJL (Nicolle chair)
21 Quai aux Fleurs
75004 Paris, France
www.chaises-nicolle.fr

Steelcase Global Headquarters
901 44th Street SE
Grand Rapids, MI 49508 USA
www.steelcase.com

Tecnolumen Gmbh & Co.KG
(Buquet lamp)
Lötzener Str. 2-4
28207 Bremen, Germany
+49 421 430 417 0
www.tecnolumen.com

Thonet Gmbh
Michael-Thonet-Strasse 1
35066 Frankenberg, Germany
+49 6451 508 0
www.thonet.de

Tolix Steel Design
Z.I Saint-Andoche Bd. Bernard Giberstein
71402 Autun Cedex, France
+33 3 85 86 96 70
www.tolix.fr

Vitra (Jean Prouvé designs)
29 Ninth Avenue
New York, NY 10014 USA
212 463 5750
www.vitra.com

BIBLIOGRAPHY

Francastel, Pierre. *Art et technique aux XIXe et XXe siècles.* Paris: Collection Tel / Gallimard, 1988.

Kaufmann, Jr., Edgar. *What Is Modern Design?* New York: Museum of Modern Art, 1954.

Teissonnière, Didier. *La Lampe Gras.* Paris: Norma Éditions, 2008.

Woronoff, Denis. *La France industrielle: Gens des ateliers et des usines, 1890–1950.* Paris: Editions du Chêne, 2003.

ACKNOWLEDGMENTS

MISHA DE POTESTAD: I would like to extend my heartfelt thanks to everyone who offered a portion of their time, shared their knowledge, and opened the doors of their workshops, houses, and archives.

At the forefront of highlighting this heritage, antiquarians Gilles Oudin and Jérôme Lepert encouraged and enabled the creation of this book. They paved the way for "industrial archeology" fifteen years ago and their collections feature here prominently.

The integration of this unique furniture in everyday settings is elegantly illustrated throughout the pages of this book, thanks to the inspired interior designs of Jean-Marc Dimanche, Paola Navone, Michel Peraches, Eric Miele, Martine Valli, Frédéric Winkler, and the brilliant and innovative work found in the showrooms of Eric Chambrion (Les Nouveaux Brocanteurs), Sylvie Château and Delphine Errakli (Objets en Transit), Véronique Chevalier and Ludovic Messager (Quintessence and Vanity Lifestyle), Frédéric Daniel (Zut!), Ghislain Bourgeois (Ghislain Antiques), and Stéphane Quatresous (Atelier 154).

I thank Jean-Luc Colonna d'Istria and Daniel Rosenztroch for access to the multiple resources available in the concept store Merci. The photos taken at this venue epitomize the new interest in industrial furniture.

Access to valuable archives and working with caring collaborators have enriched the content of this book; for this I thank Jenny Arnould (Mobilier Industriel Jérôme Lepert), Julie Blum (Galerie Anne-Sophie Duval), Framboise and Claude Cardinael (Galerie Duo), Elisabeth Cordoliani (Banque de France), Solenne de la Fouchardière (Ochre), Didier Hibert (Café L'Institut), Philippe Jousse and Remi Gerbeau (Galerie Jousse), Jacques Sautereau (Unic archives), and Jean-Yves Vergara (Lepaute archives).

I thank, for their help, the collectors Marc Hotermans and Imre Varga.

The archives of the Institut National de la Propriété Industrielle (National Industrial Property Institute) allowed me access to patents, thereby penetrating the heart of the creative process. I thank Valerie Marchal and Marie-Claude Delmas for opening the doors to this rich heritage.

A special thanks to Daniel Melamud and his team for wisely supporting this project until completion.

PATRICE PASCAL: I join Misha de Potestad in thanking all those who in one way or another have believed in our project and helped us.

I would like to thank Misha for coming up with the idea for this book and the courage to bring it to fruition.

CREDITS

Texts and styling by Misha de Potestad. All photographs are by Patrice Pascal except pp. 14–15 by Nicolas Matheus, pp. 22–23 by Stephen Clement, pp. 82–83 by Philippe de Potestad, and p. 146 by Ian Scigliuozzi.

pp. 2 (detail), 34, 35, 54, 55, 78, 106, 116, 119, 129, 158, 208 (top), 212, 214, 215 photographed at Atelier 154.

pp. 40 (top), 91, 102 (left), 103 (right), 184, 185, 187 photographed at Ghislain Antiques.

pp. 9, 10, 12, 19, 21, 26, 27, 29, 38, 42, 43, 46, 61, 62, 65, 66, 79, 81, 85, 88, 93 (right), 99 (top), 105, 110, 113, 115, 117, 118, 126, 133, 135, 136, 159, 161, 162, 164–165, 167, 170, 171, 172–173, 176, 178, 182, 188 (right), 194–195, 196, 199, 200, 201, 202, 209, 216–217 photographed at Jérôme Lepert.

pp. 73 (bottom), 102, 103 (center), 107, 108, 154, 155, 190 photographed at Les Nouveaux Brocanteurs.

pp. 75, 76, 77, 163, 186, 189, 191, 198 photographed at Objets en Transit.

pp. 16, 17, 25, 40 (bottom), 72, 99 (bottom), 138, 142, 147 (left), 156, 157, 175, 188 (left), 197, 203 (bottom), 204, 205, 208 (bottom) photographed at Gilles Oudin.

pp. 13, 41, 64, 120, 123, 144, 145, 166, 168, 169, 183, 206, 207, 213 photographed at Michel Peraches–Eric Miele.

pp. 98, 101, 121 photographed at Quintessence.

p. 109 photographed at Jean-Charles Ribes.

pp. 180, 181 photographed at Zut!

pp. 4, 143: Patent No. 254.972, "Improvements in or Relating to Supports for Electric Lamps." Louis Didier des Gachons, December 14, 1925. Courtesy of Institut National de la Propriété Industrielle (INPI), Paris.

pp. 16, 112: From Matériel pour l'Industrie [Equipment for industry], Mestre & Blatgé catalogue. Private collection.

p. 18: Patent No. 926.150, "Dispositif nouveau pour réglage en hauteur et profondeur des dossiers de sieges [New device for adjusting the height and depth of seatbacks]." Établissements Bienaise, April, 30, 1946. Courtesy of INPI.

p. 24: Patent No. 2335119, "Amélioration d'un siège [Improving a seat]." Singer Company, September 2, 1925. Courtesy of INPI.

p. 28: Établissements Jouan medical supply catalogue, 1933. Courtesy of Assistance publique–Hôpitaux de Paris (AP-HP).

p. 39: Patent No. 1.408.114, "Chair, Table and the Like." Joseph Mathieu, July 13, 1920. Courtesy of INPI.

p. 46: Blueprint for the Nicolle chair. Courtesy of Société Mobilier Industriel Jérôme Lepert (MIJL).

p. 49: "Patent drawings in the name of Mart Stam, 1929." Courtesy of Thonet.

p. 56: Patent No. 1.024.060, "Meuble tel que chaise ou meuble similaire [Furniture such as a chair or similar]." Company Mullca, March 27, 1953. Courtesy of INPI.

pp. 68, 69, 70: Jean Prouvé works pictured in photographs © 2014 Artists Rights Society (ARS), New York / ADAGP, Paris.

p. 73: "Equipement de bureaux: art et technique [Office equipment: art and technology]." Établissements Artec. Private collection.

p. 74: Ferdinand Darnay, ed. Le bureau modern [The modern office]. 1931. Private collection.

p. 76: Patent No. 54.606, "Table à dessiner [Drafting table]." Lucien Sautereau, March 6, 1942. Courtesy of INPI.

p. 80: "La table à dessin Mappemonde [The Mappemonde drafting table]." 1933. Private collection.

p. 84: Patent No. 24685, "Perfectionnements apportés dans l'établissement des tables à dessin [Improvements made in the design of the drafting table]." Maurice Leduc and Ferdinand Darnay, September 28, 1922. Courtesy of INPI.

pp. 90, 92, 93, 94, 95: Forges de Strasbourg catalogue, 1926. Private collection.

p. 104: Patent No. 659.113, "Serrure de sécurité perfectionnées [Advanced locking mechanism]." Société Fermière des coffres-forts Bauche, August 17, 1928. Courtesy of INPI.

pp. 128, 134: Patent No. 569.688, "Verrerie prismatique pour l'éclairage des rues [Prismatic glass for street lighting]." Holophane S.A. France, November 8, 1923. Courtesy of INPI, Paris.

p. 132: Patent No. 563.836, "Globe Lamp." André Blondel and Spiridon Psaroudaki, July 14, 1896. Courtesy of INPI.

p. 139: Advertisement for the Gras lamp, 1922. Private collection.

p. 147: From Lampe Ajustable [Adjustable lamp], R.A.V.E.L. catalogue. Courtesy of DCW.

p. 148: Gras lamp by Eileen Gray. Courtesy of Galerie Anne Sophie Duval.

pp. 152, 153: Lamp and patent for George Carwardine, Anglepoise. Courtesy of Anglepoise.

p. 203 (left): "Meubles en acier–Rayonnages [Steel Furniture–Shelving]." Strafor catalogue. Private collection.

First published in the United States of America in 2014 by
Rizzoli International Publications, Inc.
300 Park Avenue South
New York, NY 10010
www.rizzoliusa.com

Editor: Daniel Melamud
Design: Louise Brody
Production: Susan Lynch
Translation: Elizabeth G. Heard
Copyeditor: Elizabeth Smith
Proofreader: Rachel Selekman

Library of Congress Control Number: 2014936626
ISBN-13: 978-0-8478-4232-2

2014 2015 2016 2017 / 10 9 8 7 6 5 4 3 2 1
Printed in China